A Political Economy of American Hegemony

In *A Political Economy of American Hegemony,* Thomas Oatley explores how America's military buildups have produced postwar economic booms that have culminated in monetary and financial crises. The 2008 subprime crisis – as well as the housing bubble that produced it – was the most recent manifestation of this buildup, boom, and bust cycle, developing as a consequence of the decision to deficit finance the wars in Afghanistan and Iraq. Earlier instances of financial crises were generated by deficit-financed buildups in the 1980s and the late 1960s. The buildup, boom, and bust pattern results from the way political institutions and financial power shape America's response to military challenges: political institutions transform increased military spending into budget deficits, and financial power enables the United States to finance these deficits by borrowing cheaply from the rest of the world. Oatley examines how this cycle has had a powerful impact on American and global economic and financial performance.

Thomas Oatley teaches international politics at the University of North Carolina at Chapel Hill. He has published his scholarly work in many of the field's best journals, including *International Organization*, the *American Journal of Political Science,* and *International Studies Quarterly*. Dr. Oatley has also written two market-leading textbooks on international political economy, edited a handbook on the political economy of the international monetary system, and written a number of commentaries on contemporary affairs that have been published in outlets such as *Foreign Policy* and the *Washington Post*.

A Political Economy of American Hegemony

Buildups, Booms, and Busts

THOMAS OATLEY

University of North Carolina, Chapel Hill

CAMBRIDGE
UNIVERSITY PRESS

CAMBRIDGE
UNIVERSITY PRESS

32 Avenue of the Americas, New York, NY 10013-2473, USA

Cambridge University Press is part of the University of Cambridge.

It furthers the University's mission by disseminating knowledge in the pursuit of education, learning, and research at the highest international levels of excellence.

www.cambridge.org
Information on this title: www.cambridge.org/9781107462809

First published 2015

Printed in the United States of America

A catalog record for this publication is available from the British Library.

Library of Congress Cataloging in Publication Data
Oatley, Thomas H., 1962–
A political economy of American hegemony : buildups, booms, and busts / Thomas Oatley.
   pages   cm
Includes bibliographical references and index.
ISBN 978-1-107-09064-4 (hardback) – ISBN 978-1-107-46280-9 (paperback)
1. United States – Defenses – Economic aspects.   2. Military policy – United States.
3. Global Financial Crisis, 2008–2009.   4. Business cycles – United States.
5. United States – Foreign economic relations.   6. Globalization – Economic aspects.   I. Title.
HC110.D4O18   2015
338.4'735500973–dc23   2014038213

ISBN 978-1-107-09064-4 Hardback
ISBN 978-1-107-46280-9 Paperback

Contents

Tables and Figures

Tables

Figures

Acknowledgments

I wish to thank those who have been especially important to the genesis and success of this project. Andrew Pennock encouraged me to begin to articulate and evaluate the central thesis I present here; I doubt I would have done so without his encouragement. Susan Sell was so kind to host me as a visiting scholar at the Institute for Global and International Studies (IGIS) at George Washington University's Elliott School of International Affairs in the fall of 2009 as I conducted research for some early drafts of this project and again during the summers of 2010 and 2011. IGIS offered an ideal environment for beginning a new project: my affiliation exposed me to ideas that have influenced this project, provided a supportive environment within which to apply these ideas to my work, and allowed me to form relationships that continue to shape my thinking.

Others have provided me with valuable opportunities to present early drafts of some chapters. Dan Drezner and Kathleen McNamara provided me the opportunity to explore the central elements of American financial power in the context of a collaborative project on international financial orders, and William Grimes offered very helpful comments on my contribution. Jana Grittersova provided me the opportunity to present my argument to a group of scholars and diplomats at the Paul Nitze School of Advanced International Studies. Jonathan Kirshner provided the chance to present some of this work at Cornell University. These opportunities forced me to sharpen the argument and to focus greater attention on the underlying causal mechanisms.

A few friends and colleagues have been gracious enough to read early versions of the chapters and suggest how to improve them. Terry Sullivan has read every chapter at least once, and some many times. His understanding of executive–legislative bargaining and spatial models, as well as his deep knowledge of the Johnson administration, have improved this work immensely. My colleague Lars Shoultz read and offered helpful advice on a very early draft of the book. William Kindred Winecoff has read multiple drafts of the book, from its earliest incarnation to its final form, and asked his graduate students to read the penultimate draft. The comments were unfailingly useful and enabled me to address weaknesses in theory and evidence.

Finally, I thank Robert Dreesen at Cambridge University Press and the anonymous reviewers for the Press for giving their time to read an early and incomplete draft and offer insightful and constructive thoughts about how I could improve it.

The Political Economy of Imbalance

I think everybody wants to get to the bottom of why this happened. What were the failures of regulation? Was it regulatory negligence? Was it regulations were not sufficient?[1]

Steny Hoyer

The fall of 2008 was momentous for the United States. Financial instability that had been simmering just beneath the crust of a deflating property bubble since the summer of 2007 erupted with full force in September. In a short span of time, the U.S. government took over Fannie Mae and Freddie Mac, the two government-sponsored entities that guaranteed half of all outstanding mortgage debt. Lehman Brothers was allowed to enter bankruptcy, Merrill Lynch was acquired by Bank of America, Washington Mutual was rendered insolvent and sold to JP Morgan, and Wells Fargo acquired Wachovia. Many of the banks that survived did so only because the federal government enacted an emergency $750 billion Toxic Asset Relief Program (TARP) that enabled rapid recapitalization, and the Federal Reserve Bank purchased mortgage-backed securities in unlimited amounts. As investors panicked in the face of the apparent meltdown of the American financial system, normally liquid credit markets froze and the crisis expanded into Europe. In all, some twenty-eight countries experienced systemic banking crises in 2008 and 2009. The financial crisis thus clearly marked the end of the credit boom that had driven the housing bubble through much of the previous five years.

---

[1] Quoted in Phillips (2009).

In mid-November of that same year, the U.S. and Iraqi governments signed a Status of Forces Agreement by which the United States committed to remove its combat troops from Iraqi cities by June 30, 2009 and to withdraw all U.S. forces from Iraq by the end of 2011. The U.S. ambassador to Iraq and the Iraqi foreign minister signed the agreement in mid-November, and then President George W. Bush traveled to Baghdad in December for a formal signing ceremony. The agreement thus brought to an end the largest and costliest military action that the United States had undertaken as part of the Bush administration's broader War on Terror. The occasion was marked by a December 14, 2008 press conference in Baghdad, at which President Bush was forced to duck two shoes thrown at his head by a disgruntled Iraqi. It is not much of an exaggeration to suggest that the financial crisis and the withdrawal from Iraq combined to mark a postwar low in global perceptions of American power.

And although the housing bubble that generated the financial crisis and the War on Terror traced a common trajectory and arrived at the same destination at practically the same moment, we typically assume that they traveled along parallel tracks. The housing bubble was a consequence of poor risk management practices by private financial institutions and bad regulatory policy by government agencies. To the extent that the crisis had a global dimension, it too was financial and lay in the emergence of the global savings glut at the turn of the century. The authoritative Financial Crisis Inquiry Commission (FCIC) final report, for instance, makes no mention of the War on Terror, Iraq, or Osama bin Laden (Financial Crisis Inquiry Commission 2011). Indeed, the report does not even consider whether broader macroeconomic factors could have contributed to the crisis. The causes of the financial crisis, according to the FCIC, were entirely financial. We treat the war in Iraq as well as the broader War on Terror as a national security matter that had no discernible impact on contemporaneous economic and financial developments. And though the increased military spending arising from the War on Terror may have contributed to a federal budget deficit, the primary impact of the deficit is to bequeath a larger debt to future generations and perhaps to constrain America's ability to project military power in the near term. The contemporaneous consequences of the War on Terror are entirely measurable in terms of national security.

This book argues that the War on Terror and the housing bubble ran along the same rail. The housing bubble and the financial crisis to which it gave rise emerged as a consequence of the U.S. government's decision to pay for the War on Terror by borrowing rather than by raising taxes. The book develops this argument in the context of a broader examination of the political economy of American hegemony. The study's motivating question is straightforward: How has the military dimension of American hegemony shaped the global political economy? The question is clearly important. Military spending has consumed about 6 percent of American income, on average, each year since 1950, an amount equal to 1 to 2 percent of world income. Moreover, the defense budget has been the single largest category of U.S. government expenditures across this period, accounting for between one-quarter and one-half of all government spending. Because military spending is so large a share of total government spending, military buildups have been the single most important source of sudden, large, and persistent changes in U.S. government spending across the postwar period.

Postwar military buildups have constituted large economic events – they have increased government spending on average by roughly 2 percent of gross domestic product (GDP) for four or more consecutive years. To put this in context, consider that the American Recovery and Reinvestment Act (ARRA), enacted in February 2009 as an economic stimulus package to combat the Great Recession, increased government spending by $230 billion, or approximately 1.5 percent of GDP, in 2009 and 2010 (Congressional Budget Office 2013). The entire ARRA stimulus package, including tax cuts and expenditures after 2010, was less than 6 percent of GDP and spread out over a ten-year period. The typical postwar military buildup thus has had a proportionately larger and more sustained impact on government expenditures than the fiscal stimulus enacted to combat America's deepest postwar recession. It is quite reasonable to suppose, therefore, that the military dimension of American hegemony has had powerful economic consequences. And yet, the economic impact of America's military buildups has attracted remarkably limited attention from academics, policymakers, and the media.

The Pattern

The book asserts that the military dimension of American hegemony has repeatedly pushed a distinctive "political economy of imbalance" to the center of the global political economy. The political economy of imbalance is a cycle that has emerged each time the United States has embarked on a deficit-financed military buildup in response to an unexpected military challenge. This repeating cycle is evident in Figure 1.1,

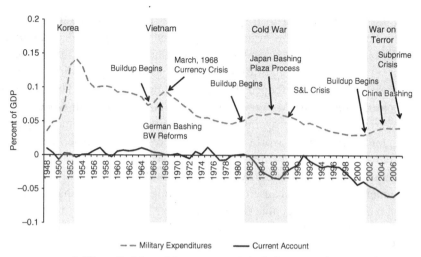

FIGURE 1.1. Military Buildups, Macroeconomic Imbalances, and Financial Crises.

which traces the evolution of the political economy of imbalance between 1950 and 2008.

Notice first that although the military's share of GDP has declined steadily across the postwar period, military spending rose sharply and persistently against this trend on four occasions. Each military buildup was triggered by a foreign event (or a sequence of foreign events in a short time span) that indicated to American policymakers that the international system was significantly more hostile to U.S. interests than policymakers had previously believed. North Korea invaded South Korea; the North Vietnamese were unexpectedly vigorous in their challenge to America's commitment to the South Vietnamese regime; the Soviets invaded Afghanistan; and al Qaeda unexpectedly hijacked commercial aircraft and crashed them into the Twin Towers and the Pentagon. Policymakers increased military spending in response to each of these foreign challenges by about 2 percent of GDP, and each military buildup persisted for three to four years.

Three of the four military buildups generated economic booms characterized by unbalanced growth. In Figure 1.1 the buildup-induced economic booms are shaded in gray and the associated economic imbalances are traced via the evolution of the current account balance. In all buildups except Korea, policymakers elected to pay for the additional military spending by borrowing rather than by raising taxes. And in all three of these deficit-financed military buildups, the resulting fiscal stimulus was pro-cyclical, adding demand to an economy already in the midst of the expansionary phase of the business cycle. The large and persistent budget deficits thus combined with existing investment and consumption expenditures to push total national expenditures well above national income. The capital inflows that financed the increased expenditures strengthened the dollar, and the stronger dollar eroded the competitiveness of the manufacturing industry.

With manufacturing competitiveness falling but the economy booming, investment and workers shifted into activities that were sheltered from international trade. Real estate construction and financial services, especially mortgage financing, were important, though certainly not the sole beneficiaries of this shift. Over the course of two of the economic booms (the Vietnam War boom was distinctive in ways I describe later in this chapter), activity in real estate construction and finance rose sharply, while manufacturing sector activity declined. And like the military build-ups that triggered them, these episodes of unbalanced growth persisted for three to four years.

The economic imbalances drove the politics of economic policy in the United States and in the global arena. In the United States, the over-valued dollar and rising imports generated a surge of protectionism. Manufacturing industries and organized labor pressured Congress and turned to administrative agencies to seek temporary relief from the intensified foreign competition. Congress responded to this growing pressure by becoming increasingly protectionist. Individual legislators and congressional committees threatened to enact legislation that would restrict imports from countries that the United States Trade Representative identified as unfair traders unless their governments removed the offending practices. Congress pressured the Treasury Department to label governments "currency manipulators" and to threaten to restrict their access to the U.S. market in order to compel policy changes.

In the global arena, the administration responded to the rise of protectionism in Congress by engaging America's trade partners in negotiations intended to reduce America's trade deficit. America's creditors have been reluctant participants in these talks, engaging in negotiations primarily because they fear that refusal to do so would lead to congressionally imposed trade sanctions. These talks targeted specific trade barriers believed to restrict U.S. firms' market access, they focused on undervalued exchange rates that undermined American competitiveness, and they sought changes in macroeconomic policies to encourage consumption in the surplus countries. Through these negotiations, the U.S. government thus sought to push the burden of adjustment necessary to narrow "global imbalances" onto its creditors. America's creditors were generally reluctant to concede in the face of American pressure. They have viewed trade imbalances as a reflection of American fiscal policy rather than a result of specific industrial or exchange rate policies they pursue at home. Creditors have seen little benefit in increasing consumption at home, and most have resisted U.S. efforts to alter currency values. The political struggle over who should bear the cost of reducing global imbalances thus produced very little adjustment. As a result, the large global imbalances were allowed to persist for the length of the boom.

Each episode was brought to a close by a major financial crisis. The Vietnam War buildup led directly to an extended dollar crisis. Foreigners accumulated substantial claims against U.S. gold reserves even as total U.S. gold reserves fell. The currency crisis began once investors recognized that devaluation of the dollar against gold was inevitable, and speculative attacks against the dollar occurred whenever investors believed dollar devaluation was imminent. The two subsequent military buildups produced the savings and loan crisis and the subprime crisis. The shift of investment into real estate generated positive feedback: rising real estate prices attracted investment, and the shift of demand into the real estate sector pushed prices up further and thereby attracted additional investment. Positive feedback fueled the emergence of real estate bubbles, and over the course of the boom the banking system became increasingly exposed to overvalued real estate. The banking system suffered a systemic crisis when the bubbles deflated.

The military dimension of American hegemony has thus repeatedly pushed the political economy of imbalance to the center of the global economy. Buildups have generated economic booms; the resulting economic imbalances have sparked political conflict over trade and exchange rate policies. Over the course of the boom, financial imbalances accumulated and ultimately led to financial instability. This book argues that this political economy of imbalance has been a central characteristic of American hegemony and develops an explanation that helps us understand why it has been so.

The Argument

Why has American hegemony been characterized by this political economy of imbalance? In broad terms, I argue that the political economy of imbalance has been pushed to the center of the global economy by the interaction between America's domestic political institutions and its international financial power. America's political institutions channel the American policy response to unexpected foreign military challenges – what I call security shocks. These institutions enable policymakers to increase military spending quickly in response to the threat, but they also greatly restrict the ability to raise taxes or reduce spending on social welfare programs. As a consequence, the U.S. government has paid for most postwar military buildups by borrowing. America's financial power enables the United States to borrow from the rest of the world in large volumes, for extended periods, at low interest rates. The willingness of the rest of the world to lend to American borrowers ensures that the budget deficits generated by America's military buildups do not crowd out domestic investment or reduce private consumption. In combination, America's political institutions and financial power transform security shocks into a persistent, pro-cyclical fiscal stimulus that fuels booms and generates economic and financial imbalances.

American Political Institutions

American political institutions divide and decentralize political authority. At the broadest level, this division of authority is a consequence of the constitutionally mandated separation of powers that establishes the executive and legislative branches as independent bodies. The constitutional separation of powers is accentuated by a functional separation of power in the Congress imparted by the members' commitment to the committee system. The decentralization is perhaps further strengthened by relatively weak party discipline in an electoral system that creates strong incentives for each individual legislator to attach greater weight to the specific interests of district residents than to the broader concerns of the party as a whole. The decentralization of authority creates a political process in which policy choices must be negotiated between autonomous actors in Congress and the executive branch, as well as between the two houses of Congress, rather than selected and implemented authoritatively by an executive with an assured legislative majority.

This decentralized political system is prone to gridlock. Because departures from the status quo require the consent of a large number of veto players, the ability to shift policy quickly requires veto players' preferences to be homogeneous (Binder 1999; Binder 2003; Klarner, Phillips, and Muckler 2012; McCubbins 1991). Yet, because veto players represent diverse interests across a large geographic area, hold different views about

the appropriate role of government in society, and adhere to distinct ideological orientations, the probability that all of them will prefer the same
policy stance all the time is relatively low. Hence, the institutional structure tends to produce heterogeneous veto player preferences that impart
a strong status quo bias to policy outcomes. Once politicians negotiate a
policy outcome, subsequent movement away from that outcome requires
substantial and convergent change of veto players' preferences.

Of course, policy does not remain locked into a single outcome forever. But when change does occur, it often occurs suddenly and shifts
policy significantly. Existing research characterizes these dynamics of policy change in terms of punctuated equilibrium (Baumgartner et al. 2009;
Baumgartner and Jones 1993; Jones and Baumgartner 2005; Jones et al.
2009). In a political system characterized by punctuated equilibrium an
extended period of policy stability gives way to an abrupt and large policy change and then settles back into an extended period of policy stability. The underlying causal dynamics revolve around competing forces.
On the one hand, changes in the social environment produce a steady
accumulation of pressure for policy change. On the other hand, institutions impart friction to the policy process that restricts movement away
from the status quo. Policy change occurs when the accumulated pressure is sufficient to override the institutional friction that keeps the system stable. When that threshold is crossed, the system lurches from its
current state to a new one, which can be far from the status quo ante.
Once policy has moved, institutional friction restricts further adjustment,
and the system settles back into an extended period of policy stability
(Baumgartner et al. 2009: 867).

The stickiness of policy outcomes in the American political system
transforms security shocks into large and persistent budget deficits. The
multiple veto player nature of the system constrains most year-to-year
changes in military spending to small amounts. The need to gain agreement among a large number of actors who hold different assessments
of the military threat America faces and the utility of military force as
a deterrent against this threat constrain changes in defense spending.
Sudden large changes of defense spending in this system are possible only
in response to unexpected foreign military challenges, such as the terrorist attack of September 11. Such challenges produce an immediate convergence of veto players' preferences around the need for a substantially
larger military. Yet, these security shocks have no impact on veto players'
preferences over other dimensions of the budget. Policymakers continue
to hold very different preferences over the appropriate tax rate and the

appropriate levels of social welfare spending. In the face of this heterogeneity, veto players disagree sharply about how to pay for the larger military they all agree is necessary. As a result, as previously mentioned, the United States has paid for most postwar military buildups by borrowing rather than by raising taxes.

American Financial Power

The United States can borrow rather than tax to pay for military buildups because it possesses substantial financial power. Financial power is the ability of a national economy to borrow from the rest of the world in large volumes, for an extended period, at low interest rates (Cohen 2006; Krippner 2011; see also Schwartz 2009; Strange 1989, 1998). Financial power as such inheres to the national economy as a whole. That is, financial power does not inhere solely in the ability of the *government* to borrow cheaply from the rest of the world, but lies in the ability of the economy *as a whole* to borrow cheaply from the rest of the world in large volumes and for extended periods. Thus, when we speak of American financial power, we are not speaking narrowly about the U.S. government's ability to finance a budget deficit by selling bonds to China (or Japan). Nor are we restricting our attention to monetary power; the benefits that accrue to the U.S. government from the dollar's role as the world's primary reserve currency. We are talking more broadly about the ability of all U.S. residents to sell financial assets, such as mortgage-backed securities, corporate bonds, stocks, bank deposits, as well as government bonds, to foreigners. Financial power is thus the ability to escape the "crowding out" constraint: when government borrowing increases, foreign capital rushes in to plug the gap between the increased demand for and an unchanged domestic supply of savings.

Financial power derives from the interaction between country-level attributes and the network structure of the international financial system. At the country level, "confidence" is the key factor. Confidence is fundamentally a function of credit risk and liquidity risk. Credit risk is the probability that a borrower will default. The probability of default in turn is a function of the underlying strength of the economy, which shapes the health of the corporate sector and thus the likelihood of default on corporate bonds. Default risk is a function of government reputation that shapes the probability of a sovereign default. Default risk is a function of the stability of the banking system. On all of these dimensions, the U.S. financial system scores high in absolute and relative terms: the risk of default is extremely low, as low as or lower than that of all other countries. Liquidity risk is largely a function of the size of capital markets. Many countries offer sound investment opportunities; but most markets are relatively small. The United States, in contrast, has the largest and most active capital markets in the world. The liquidity of these markets generally enables holders of dollar-denominated assets of all kinds to liquidate their holdings quickly and at low cost. Country-level characteristics combine to make the U.S. financial system the market in which credit risk and liquidity risk are very low.

Country-level characteristics are reinforced by the network structure of the international financial system. The American financial system stands at the center of the global financial network (Oatley et al. 2013). The United States attracts financial assets in larger amounts and from more countries than any other national financial system in the world. And the difference between the United States and other countries is not linear; the United States is twice as central as the second most central system (the United Kingdom), four times as the third most central (Germany and Luxembourg), and orders of magnitude more central than the tenth most central countries. America's central location in the global financial network generates positive feedback that encourages capital to flow to the United States from the rest of the world. The extent to which the United States attracts foreign capital is a positive function of the amount of foreign capital it has attracted. The willingness of foreign investors to acquire additional dollar-denominated assets is a positive function of the volume of dollar-denominated assets foreigners hold. This dynamic contrasts sharply with the capital market dynamics that apply to other countries, where the volume of capital inflows is typically a negative function of current exposure. In a sense, then, the United States has financial power in part because it already has financial power.

One sees evidence of America's financial power in the evolution of net cross border capital flows between 1970 and 2008. Figure 1.2 traces the evolution of global imbalances, as well as the cross-national distribution of these imbalances, between 1970 and 2008. The measure of global imbalance is the sum of all national current account deficits each year as a share of world GDP. Between 1975 and 2003, global imbalances varied within a relatively narrow range, between 1 and 2 percent of world GDP. After 2003, global imbalances increased sharply, almost doubling the 1975–2003 average. The measure of the cross-national distribution of these imbalances is a Gini coefficient calculated for the ten largest national current account deficits – which account for about 70 percent of the total global imbalance – in each year. This Gini coefficient rises toward

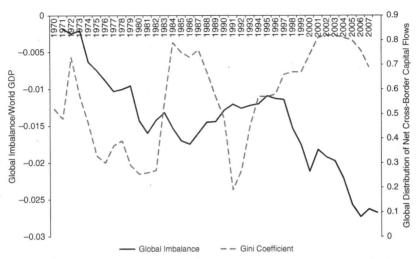

FIGURE 1.2. The Global Distribution of Net Cross-Border Capital Flows, 1970–2007.

unity as net cross-border capital flows become heavily concentrated in a single country and falls toward zero as capital flows are more evenly distributed across the ten largest deficit countries. In contrast to total imbalances, the cross-national distribution of net capital flows has varied substantially over the period, ranging from a low of 0.3 to a high of 0.85. Hence, although total net cross-border capital flows have remained fairly stable across time (at least until 2003), the degree to which these capitals have been distributed evenly across countries or concentrated heavily in a single country has varied substantially.

Variation in the cross-national distribution of net capital flows has been driven by variation in the U.S. demand for foreign capital. Figure 1.3 plots the U.S. current account deficit – the simplest measure of U.S. demand for foreign capital – against the cross-national distribution of net capital flows over the same period. The plot clearly indicates a strong positive relationship between U.S. external imbalances and the concentration of net cross-border capital flows. When the U.S. demand for foreign capital rises, it attracts an increasing share of total net cross-border capital flows. When U.S. demand for foreign capital falls, net capital flows are more evenly distributed across the world's deficit countries. At one extreme, large U.S. current account deficits are associated with a Gini coefficient of 0.82. At the other end, small U.S. current account deficits are associated with Gini coefficients that range between 0.3 and 0.5. The magnitude

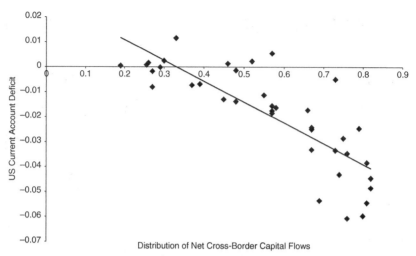

FIGURE 1.3. U.S. Imbalances and the Global Distribution of Net Cross-Border Capital Flows.

of the total global imbalance correlates with the concentration of net cross-border flows, at least since 1980 (see Figure 1.2). Global imbalances widen as net capital flows become more concentrated in the United States, and global imbalances narrow as net capital flows are more widely distributed across the system. Notice also the distinctive global environment within which the 2008 subprime crisis arose. Although the crisis was not America's first postwar banking crisis centered in real estate, it was the largest and it had a much greater global impact than the savings and loan crisis of the 1980s. Figure 1.2 suggests that this greater magnitude was a product of the convergence of two historically unprecedented trends. On the one hand, global imbalances rose to unprecedented magnitude between 1998 and 2005. On the other hand, the capital flows associated with these imbalances became concentrated in a single country, the United States, and on a single sector in that single country to an unprecedented degree as well. Thus, from 2001 to 2007, the global financial system became ever more highly vulnerable to adverse developments in American real estate.

These dynamics reflect America's financial power: when the U.S. demand for foreign capital rises, the U.S. attracts an increasing share of a growing volume of cross-border capital flows. This ensures that an increase in U.S. government borrowing doesn't crowd out investment in the American economy, but instead crowds out investment (and decreases consumption) in some other part of the world. As Greta Krippner has noted in her research on the financialization of the American economy, American "policymakers discovered ... that they lived in a world in which capital was available in a potentially limitless supply. Access to global financial markets would allow the state to defer indefinitely the difficult political choices [as it struggled] to allocate scarce capital between competing social priorities" (Krippner 2011: 101–102).

America's financial power thus allows the U.S. government to increase military spending sharply in response to foreign military challenges without needing to resolve political conflict over how to pay for it. Because the United States can import capital in large volumes at low cost for extended periods, policymakers face little diffuse market pressure to agree on deficit-reduction measures. And the ease with which the United States attracts foreign capital implies that the private sector is not facing higher borrowing costs as a result of government borrowing either. Hence, the corporate sector has little reason to pressure the government to balance the budget and the financial sector profits from intermediating the larger volume of funds flowing into the American economy. Financial power thereby enables the U.S. government to increase military spending without having to cut social welfare programs, without having to reduce private consumption, and without having to reduce private sector investment.

Capital market dynamics transform deficit-financed military buildups into asset bubbles. The classic Kindleberger-Minsky (K&M) model asserts that asset bubbles are triggered by exogenous shocks, that is, by unexpected events that originate outside the financial system (Kindleberger and Aliber 2005; Minsky 1972). Kindleberger (2005: 25–26) argues that asset bubbles "start with a 'displacement,' some exogenous, outside shock to the macroeconomic system." Many events can provide this initial displacement: a perceived productivity shock, a bumper harvest or a crop failure, and an unanticipated change in monetary policy. My focus on security shocks and the resulting fiscal policy shocks as the source of the initial displacement was anticipated by Kindleberger, who suggests that the outbreak or conclusion of wars has also sparked asset bubbles. If the shock is large and pervasive, the economic outlook and profit opportunities improve. Businesses and individuals borrow to take advantage of the heightened opportunities. Optimism in turn creates positive feedback, pulling additional investment using borrowed funds into the favored sector. Positive feedback via the financial system thus amplifies the impact of the initial fiscal impulse, generating the asset bubble and, eventually, financial instability.

The political economy of imbalance thus emerges from the way America's political institutions and its global financial power channel the policy response to security shocks. Unexpected foreign military challenges prompt American policymakers to increase military spending substantially. America's political institutions transform these military buildups into large and persistent budget deficits by allowing policymakers to increase military spending but constraining their ability to change tax rates or social welfare spending. America's financial power enables the U.S. government to finance the resulting budget deficits without paying high interest rates or crowding out private investment or consumption. As a result, military buildups sparked by unexpected foreign challenges impart a powerful, persistent, and typically pro-cyclical fiscal stimulus to the U.S. economy that gives rise to the political economy of imbalance.

The Political Economy of Imbalance in Broader Context

Because I causally connect events that rarely find themselves connected, it is useful – and perhaps even necessary – to fit my argument into existing explanations of the subprime crisis in particular and asset bubbles and banking crises more generally. The most commonly advanced explanation of the subprime crisis focuses on the growing complexity of the American financial system and the increasingly market-oriented character of American financial regulations (see, e.g., Financial Crisis Inquiry Commission 2011; Helleiner 2011; Helleiner, Pagliari, and Zimmerman 2010; Johnson and Kwak 2010; McCarty, Poole, and Rosenthal 2013; Moschella and Tsingou 2013; Mosley and Singer 2009; Roubini and Mihm 2010; Seabrooke and Tsingou 2010; Thompson 2009; Tsingou 2010). Growing financial complexity is seen to have been a consequence of increased reliance on "new models of securitization," and in particular on the increased importance of mortgaged backed securities (MBS) and collateralized debt obligations (CDOs) (Helleiner 2011: 71).

Securitization is held to have had two pernicious consequences for financial system stability. First, securitization created a substantial gap between the firms that originate mortgages and the firms that ultimately hold them as assets in their portfolios. Because originators did not keep mortgages on their balance sheets for very long, and because they made money from origination fees, they benefited by generating a large number of new mortgages and had relatively little concern with the long-run creditworthiness of the borrowers. Second, the bundling and re-bundling of mortgages into tradable securities made it increasingly difficult for market participants to fully evaluate the risk attached to the assets they held. Credit rating agencies made it easy to neglect this complexity by rating these securities as low-risk or investment grade securities. These factors combined to diminish the incentive and the ability of financial institutions to manage more effectively the risk that increasingly dominated their balance sheets.

Regulatory structures are viewed to have done too little to discourage these practices and to require the relevant financial institutions to hold sufficient capital to protect them in the event of an adverse shock. Many point to financial deregulation in the United States in the late 1990s as a turning point. The Financial Services Modernization Act of 1999 removed the firewall between commercial and investment banking that the Glass-Steagall Act of 1933 had inserted, thereby enabling commercial banks to participate in the securitization of mortgages and other securities. The enthusiasm for deregulation was accompanied by a belief in self-regulation. Within the banking sector, regulators encouraged banks to employ their internal value-at-risk models to calculate the capital necessary to cover their overall credit risk (Helleiner 2011: 72). Outside of the banking sector, financial institutions were encouraged to work through private associations to develop and apply common standards and practices. And where governments did take the lead to create international financial regulation, such as with the Basel Accords on bank capital, the resulting rules applied only to commercial banks, and not to the shadow banking system where the behaviors that generated the crisis were most common. Overall, therefore, the period is seen as one in which regulators placed too much faith in the ability of the large financial institutions to manage risk effectively and prudently. As former Chairman of the Federal Reserve Board Alan Greenspan told the House Committee on Oversight and Government Reform in October, 2008, "Those of us who have looked to the self-interest of lending institutions to protect shareholders' equity, myself included, are in a state of shocked disbelief" (Andrews 2008: B1).

Conventional wisdom thus holds that deepening financial complexity combined with regulatory laxity to generate the real estate bubble and ensuing banking crisis. As the Obama administration's FCIC concluded, "The captains of finance and the public stewards of our financial system ignored warnings and failed to question, understand, and manage evolving risks ... Theirs was a big miss, not a stumble" (Financial Crisis Inquiry

Commission 2011: xvii). The principal shortcoming of this conventional account is that emphasis on specific characteristics of American financial practices and regulatory structures during the 2000s overlooks similarities between the subprime crisis and the larger set of real estate bubbles and banking crises that have occurred since the mid-1970s. Eighteen systemic banking crises occurred in advanced industrialized countries between 1977 and 2007 (Reinhart and Rogoff 2008a). These eighteen crises exhibit two similarities. First, each country experienced a substantial net inflow of foreign capital in the three years preceding the banking crisis; and second, these capital inflows generated a real estate bubble in the three years that preceded each crisis (Bordo and Jeanne 2002; Gerdrup 2003; Reinhart and Reinhart 2009). If we expand the sample to include emerging market countries we find that generally a 1 percent increase in net capital inflows has been associated with a 10 percent increase in real estate prices (Aizenman and Jinjarak 2009). The subprime crisis exhibits identical traits: net capital inflows increased by 3 percent of GDP, and real estate prices increased nationwide by 30 percent. The U.S. subprime crisis is fully consistent with a broader pattern, even if in magnitude it lies in the right tail of the distribution. This suggests that conventional wisdom might weigh the idiosyncratic components of the subprime crisis too heavily and accord too little weight to factors common across a larger sample of postwar banking crises.

I reverse this typical weighting, attaching greater significance to factors common across banking crises and less importance to specific elements evident only in the subprime crisis. And in doing so I attach greatest weight to the macroeconomic imbalances out of which bubbles and banking crises generally have emerged. My focus on macroeconomic imbalances is shared by an increasing number of prominent economists. Global imbalances first received significant attention in a 2005 speech by then Chairman of the Federal Reserve Board Ben Bernanke. Bernanke argued that high savings rates in East Asia (in China especially) and in oil exporting countries were creating large global imbalances (Bernanke 2005; Bernanke et al. 2011; Claessens et al. 2010; Dell'Ariccia et al. 2013; Justiniano, Primiceri, and Tambalotti 2013; Obstfeld and Rogoff 2009). This "global savings glut" hypothesis attaches primary causal importance to the quest for high-quality, low-risk, dollar-denominated assets by the high savings societies. As noted above, however, most postwar banking crises have emerged in the context of rising capital inflows, and all occurred well before the global savings glut emerged. A global savings glut explanation thus shares the same limitation as work that emphasizes securitization and regulatory laxity – excessive emphasis on what is unique to the subprime crisis and too little attention to how it is similar to other crises. Moreover, though the global savings glut helps us understand the magnitude of the subprime crisis relative to other banking crises, we need to examine the factors that drive variation in the U.S. demand for foreign capital if we wish to explain why these savings were attracted to the United States rather than distributed more evenly across the world.

Political economists have been reluctant to embrace explanations of the subprime crisis rooted in macroeconomic imbalances, preferring instead explanations centered on characteristics of the financial system. *Lost Decade* (2011), co-written by Menzie Chinn and Jeff Frieden, along with Herman Schwartz's *Subprime Nation* (2009), are two prominent exceptions. Chinn and Frieden treat the subprime crisis as a debt-driven consumption boom that we can understand by embedding it in the context of debt-driven booms and busts that have occurred elsewhere. And they attach substantial causal significance to the Bush administration's 2001 tax cut and the resulting government budget deficits. Chinn and Frieden thus offer an explanation that is similar to the argument I develop here, one based firmly on a standard open economy approach to current account deficits, capital flows, and exchange rate movements. My argument differs from theirs in three important ways. First, I attach more importance to sudden large changes in military spending than to tax cuts. Second, whereas Chinn and Frieden stress a continuity that they see in American debt dependence since the 1980s, I argue that America's reliance on foreign debt has been cyclical rather than secular. Third, I am more explicit about how American political institutions shape the fiscal policy response to exogenous shocks.

Herman Schwartz develops an explanation of the American housing bubble centered on the structure of contemporary global trade and financial flows and the position of the American financial system within this structure. He argues that the crisis arose out of the way that American financial institutions recycled China's trade surplus. American financiers borrowed on short term at low interest from China and other high savings societies, transformed these loans into mortgage-backed securities, and then distributed these securities back to savers across the global economy. This arbitrage, as Schwartz calls it, imparted a Keynesian demand stimulus to the American economy as capital inflows fuelled a housing bubble that drove home prices higher, while home equity loans enabled home owners to realize these capital gains in order to finance an import-intensive consumption boom. My argument shares some characteristics with Schwartz's explanation, especially the focus on the Keynesian stimulus imparted to the American economy by rising capital inflows.

My argument differs from *Subprime Nation*, however, in two important ways. First, Schwartz treats the subprime crisis as a unique event, calling the crisis "a singularity" that actors created "contingently from a specific set of antecedent conditions, tools, and opportunities" (Schwartz 2009: 21). He argues that the unique character of the crisis greatly limits our ability to use the case to develop more general law-like statements about the global political economy. In contrast, I treat the subprime crisis as but one of a larger set of crises. Consequently, I believe that commonalities across America's postwar episodes of financial instability demand a common explanation, even if the explanation constitutes a historically contingent claim about the impact of American military and financial power on the postwar global political economy rather than a "law-like" statement applicable across time and space. Second, for Schwartz the bubble arose endogenously from the global economy given the structure of the system. I argue that the asset bubble was triggered by the fiscal shock imparted by the U.S. response to the attacks of September 11.

Finally, my focus on the macroeconomic dimensions of the subprime crisis links dynamics of the global financial system to the military dimension of American hegemony. A large literature argues that military burdens have weakened the American economy (Calleo 1982, 1992, 2010; Gilpin 1981; Kennedy 1987; Layne 2012; Narizny 2007; Trubowitz 2011). The logic of crowding out stands at the center of this argument: the cost of defending the hegemonic order requires taxes or debt that displace productive investment, thereby weakening economic performance. As the hegemon's economic performance deteriorates, the need to respond to foreign challenges pushes the hegemon to tax more heavily, thus further reducing investment. My argument embeds this imperial overstretch hypothesis in an open economy context, with two important consequences. First, crowding out disappears once we incorporate global finance and American financial power. This helps us understand the lack of relationship between U.S. military spending and growth (Brooks, Ikenberry, and Wohlforth 2013; Calleo 2009, 2010; Heo 2010; see, e.g., Layne 2011; see also Layne 2012). As Brooks et al. (2013: 27) summarize, "there is scant theoretical or empirical reason to link rates of growth to either the distribution of power or the specific policies the United States pursues to sustain its leadership ... No scholarly theory or empirical findings clearly link the 2007–2009 financial collapse, great recession, and consequent ballooning of the U.S. budget deficit to the international system (at least, as scholars of international security construe it). Nor does any established research finding show a connection between any U.S. security commitment and the causes of the economic downturn." But this literature has concluded incorrectly from this research that military spending has no economic consequences. I contest this conclusion by highlighting the large and persistent imbalances that deficit-financed military buildups generate.

In summary, I argue that existing explanations place too much emphasis on idiosyncratic elements of the subprime crisis. Securitization, deregulation and regulatory laxity, and the global savings glut all play important roles in the development of the asset bubble and the resulting banking crisis. Yet, the focus on these specific details obscures the many ways in which the subprime crisis was similar to the booms, bubbles, and episodes of financial instability that the United States has experienced throughout the postwar era, and it obscures the causal dynamics that these American crises share with similar crises throughout the world. By embedding the subprime crisis in the broader political economy of America's postwar hegemony, we come to understand that episodes of financial instability have emerged as a consequence of large and persistent macroeconomic imbalances that originate in the way that American political institutions and global financial power channel the political system's response to unexpected foreign military challenges.

The Approach

My epistemological approach is perhaps best characterized as analytic eclecticism (Sil and Katzenstein 2010). Analytic eclecticism is a problem oriented, integrative, and pragmatic approach to social science. Analytic eclecticism has been developed as a partial remedy for the oft-voiced concern that contemporary political science suffers from a "flight from reality"(Shapiro 2005). In the search for general knowledge, academic research has become increasingly theory driven and methods driven as it has become increasingly specialized and compartmentalized. The result is a set of research programs composed of a relatively small number of scholars who speak to each other with ever greater precision about ever more narrowly framed questions. As modern political science has evolved in this direction, professionals have spent less and less time grappling with complex substantive contemporary problems with the goal of generating practical as well as scholarly knowledge. Analytic eclecticism seeks to engage such real-world problems by integrating the work generated in separate research programs.

More specifically, Sil and Katzenstein (2010) advance three markers of eclectic scholarship. The first marker concerns problem selection and research purpose: "analytic eclecticism features the articulation or problems that reflect, rather than simplify, the complexity and multidimensionality of social phenomena of interest to both scholars and practitioners" (Sil and Katzenstein 2010: 19). In essence, this marker involves two considerations: first, eclectic research concentrates on important "real-world problems" rather than more narrowly specified dependent variables. This book's focus on the complex relationship between U.S. military spending and American financial crises certainly fits this marker closely. Second, eclectic research tries to deepen our understanding of these problems rather than test hypotheses drawn from or contribute to the development of a specific paradigm or research program. Thus, my purpose in this book is to deepen our understanding of the economic and financial consequences of America's postwar military buildups based on established mid-range theories rather than use this material to develop general or universally valid claims about the economic and financial consequences of military spending.

The second marker of analytical eclecticism concerns how it manages the complexity inherent in these real-world problems: analytic eclecticism pays "attention to the multiplicity, heterogeneity, and interaction of causal mechanisms and processes that generate" the phenomena of interest (Sil and Katzenstein 2010: 21). Thus, in contrast to paradigmatic research, which strives to reduce complexity in order to focus on narrowly specified causal relationships, analytic eclecticism embraces complexity. For Sil and Katzenstein, this approach entails openness to processes that cut across different levels of analysis as well as the interaction between different subsystems that are typically studied in isolation. This book pursues this goal by exploring the interaction between the causal mechanisms that produce outcomes for U.S. national security, fiscal policy, trade policy, and financial system stability. Finally, research conducted in this way is not intended to produce either general laws or ideographic narratives, but instead an explanation that identifies cause–effect relationships "that can, in principle, recur with some degree of frequency within contexts that possess certain conditions or characteristics relevant to the problem of phenomenon under investigation" (Sil and Katzenstein 2010: 22). I thus do suggest that the political economy of

American hegemony has been characterized by a set of cause–effect relationships that have recurred across the postwar era.

The third marker of analytic eclecticism is that research findings should speak to important contemporary social and/or policy problems. Policy relevance need not be the primary purpose of such work, but rather the research should construct "theories or narratives that generate 'pragmatic engagement' with the social conditions within which prevailing ideas about world politics have emerged" (Sil and Katzenstein 2010: 22). And as they elaborate, "even when it is not offering explicit policy prescriptions, eclectic scholarship should have some clear implications for some set of policy debates or salient normative concerns that enmesh leaders, public intellectuals, and other actors in a given political setting" (Ibid). On this dimension, my focus on the complex interaction between causal mechanisms that we typically study in isolation produces findings with relevance to how we conceptualize the causes of and thereby solutions to financial instability. The findings also encourage us to conceptualize the economic consequences of deficit-financed military buildups differently than we do typically.

Though this book hews to the principles of analytic eclecticism, my precise approach differs a bit from that which Sil and Katzenstein advocate. Sil and Katzenstein encourage the integration of causal mechanisms from different research paradigms which, in the context of international relations they define as realism, liberalism, and constructivism. Others, such as David Lake (2011, 2013), have encouraged scholars to replace these "isms" with a focus on the interests of actors interacting within institutions. Lake (2011: 473) argues that any complete theory of politics must specify these three elements, and moreover, that organizing our research around these concepts provides a common language that will enable us to combine or selectively integrate mid-range theories. My eclecticism shares much with Lake's; I focus on mid-range theories based on actors' interests, interactions, and institutions. And I integrate causal mechanisms across research programs that share a focus on these three components rather than across paradigms.

Though the external validity of my empirical findings is not my foremost consideration, the internal validity of these results work is. I thus employ a two-stage empirical strategy. First, although my explanation stresses the complex interaction between the politics of defense spending, fiscal policy, and capital market reactions, I test the causal mechanisms that I hypothesize are operative at each step of the causal sequence. Each chapter thus focuses on one stage of the causal process, such as the impact of security shock on military spending, the relationship between military spending and budget deficits, and so forth. Each chapter develops the central causal mechanism from existing theoretical and empirical research and then tests the resulting causal mechanism against the record of American postwar history.

Second, I employ a mixed methods approach to test the posited relationships. A mixed methods research approach is one in which the "investigator collects and analyzes data, integrates the findings, and draws inferences using both qualitative and quantitative approaches or methods in a single study or a program of inquiry. Its central premise is that the use of quantitative and qualitative approaches in combination provides a better understanding of research problems than either approach alone" (Creswell and Clark 2010: 5). A mixed methods approach benefits from large-n statistical analysis, especially the ability to evaluate the magnitude, significance, robustness, and generality of a hypothesized relationship. The approach then benefits from small-n qualitative analysis of individual cases to evaluate more closely the causal mechanisms hypothesized to produce the relationship. Employing this approach thus permits me to have greater confidence about the internal validity of my theoretical argument than I could achieve by relying solely on either a quantitative or a qualitative approach.

I apply this to each stage in the posited causal chain. Every chapter thus provides quantitative and qualitative evidence on the central relationships of interest. I perform a variety of statistical tests to gain confidence that my hypothesized empirical relationships are both systematic – characterized the entire postwar period rather than just parts of it – and robust to the inclusion of relevant control variables. I further enhance confidence in this correlational analysis by comparing the American experience with correlational studies conducted on a larger sample. I then turn to qualitative analysis to evaluate my hypothesized causal mechanisms. Where possible and appropriate, I rely on primary documents to examine decision-making processes. Where such evidence is lacking, I rely on secondary sources and contemporary accounts. This approach provides substantial confidence that the argument I advance is a compelling characterization of the political economy of American hegemony.

A Roadmap

I develop the political economy of imbalance over the next five chapters. I organize the book around the causal mechanisms that characterize each stage of the cycle. Each chapter articulates the theoretical logic relevant to a single stage of the political economy of imbalance and evaluates the empirical validity of the posited causal mechanism using quantitative and qualitative evidence.

Chapter 2 establishes the relationship between exogenous security shocks and changes in military spending. The chapter demonstrates first that military spending exhibits a powerful status quo bias. The overwhelming majority of year-to-year changes in military spending are very small – on the order of 1 percent or less. But on a few occasions, military spending has increased substantially – by 10 percent or more. The chapter then develops a spatial model to account for this pattern. The model asserts that uncertainty about the true military threat to American interests allows veto players to have the same objective – secure American interests – but to disagree about how much military spending is required to achieve this goal. Disagreement limits changes in military spending. Veto players' military spending preferences shift in response to security shocks. Security shocks indicate unambiguously that the threat to U.S. interests is substantially greater than previously believed, and veto players update their beliefs to incorporate this new information. As a consequence, the preferences of all veto players converge around a much larger military budget in the wake of the shock. The chapter then evaluates the theoretical model. It demonstrates first that large changes in military spending have been highly correlated with security shocks. It then presents qualitative evidence to demonstrate the validity of the hypothesized causal mechanism. In combination, the evidence strongly suggests that all postwar military buildups have occurred as reactions to exogenous security shocks. Chapter 3 establishes the budgetary consequences of postwar military buildups. The chapter first demonstrates empirically that military buildups have been the single most important cause of America's large and persistent budget deficits. The chapter then develops a spatial model to explain why military buildups generate large and persistent budget deficits. The model suggests that the budgetary impact of military buildups is a function of the heterogeneity of veto players' preferences over tax rates and social welfare spending. When preferences are homogeneous, veto players quickly increase taxes or cut social welfare spending to accommodate the increased military burden and no deficit results. When preferences are heterogeneous, political conflict makes budget adjustment difficult. The model also suggests that given heterogeneous preferences, budget deficits persist because bargaining over deficit reduction becomes fused to deeply rooted differences about the role of the state in the economy. The chapter evaluates these expectations by reconstructing congressional–executive budget bargaining in the wake of each security shock. It demonstrates that when veto players' preferences were homogeneous, policymakers paid for military buildup with higher taxes. When preferences have been heterogeneous, conflict over how to adjust yielded a large deficit that persisted as negotiations devolved into a struggle over the appropriate role of the state in the American economy.

Chapter 4 examines the macroeconomic impact of the budget deficits caused by military buildups. Drawing on a standard two-sector open economy model, the chapter first delineates the macroeconomic impact of expansionary fiscal policy in a large open economy. The model indicates that a fiscal expansion should increase output, strengthen the currency, weaken the current account, and increase net capital inflows. In addition, the model suggests that currency appreciation should cause investment and employment to flow into the non-traded sector. The chapter then evaluates these expectations against America's postwar macroeconomic record. The empirical analysis highlights a three-stage sequence through which deficit-financed military buildups have generated unbalanced growth. In stage 1, deficit-financed military buildups impart persistent pro-cyclical stimulus to the economy, and thereby transform an ongoing economic expansion into an economic boom. In stage 2, the current account worsens and net capital inflows increase. Developments in stage 3 depend upon the exchange rate regime. Under the floating exchange rate regime in place since 1973, capital inflows have strengthened the dollar and these relative price movements have encouraged investment and employment to shift out of manufacturing and into real estate, construction, financial services, and other activities sheltered from international trade. When the dollar was pegged to gold, as it was prior to 1973, the fiscal expansion forces the central bank to intervene to support the fixed exchange rate, thereby preventing a change in relative prices but reinforcing the fiscal expansion.

Chapter 5 explores the domestic political response to the macroeconomic imbalances generated by deficit-financed military buildups. The chapter argues that these imbalances spark a rise of protectionism centered in Congress and bargaining over adjustment with surplus economies. Protectionism arises because of the impact of the over-valued dollar on the international competitiveness of American manufacturing. Manufactured goods producers react to their declining fortunes by pressuring Congress for higher tariffs, administrative barriers, and exchange rate changes. The congressional response to private industry pressure eventually prompts the White House to embark on negotiations with the large surplus economies. Through these negotiations, American policy-makers leverage foreign dependence on American economic and military power to push some of the costs of current account adjustment onto the surplus states via changes in their trade barriers, currency values, and macroeconomic policies.

Chapter 6 examines the financial consequences of large and persistent imbalances. The chapter argues that the precise form of the financial consequences have been conditioned by the exchange rate regime in place during the buildup. Under the floating rate regime in place since 1973, sustained imbalances have generated real estate bubbles and banking crises: the savings and loan crisis of 1988 and the subprime crisis of 2008. Under a fixed exchange rate, imbalances produced an extended dollar crisis. In addition, the chapter presents evidence to demonstrate that these American crises traced the paths of banking and currency crises elsewhere in the global economy, and that the United States has experienced these crises only in the context of buildup-induced booms.

Chapter 7 considers what the research reported here implies for post-crisis and postwar American policy. I argue that current policy relies too narrowly on new financial regulations to try to prevent future crises, and relies too heavily on retrenchment to rejuvenate American power. Instead, reducing the likelihood of future crises and restoring American global influence requires transition to a strategy of "responsible global engagement" – an engagement that relies less on military power, and pays for the military power it does use out of current income.

Conclusion

The military dimension of American hegemony has pushed the political economy of imbalance to the center of the global economy. Military build-ups have triggered economic booms. Booms have given rise to large and persistent macroeconomic imbalances and price distortions. Financing this unbalanced growth for extended periods has led to accumulating financial fragilities that ultimately produced major episodes of financial instability. This dynamic has been a product of how America's political institutions and its financial power have shaped the policy response to security shocks. The War on Terror, the housing bubble, and the sub-prime crisis were the most recent manifestations of this broader pattern of America's postwar hegemony.

These buildups, booms, imbalances, and busts have structured the evolution of global political economy in ways that are not widely appreciated. The economic booms generated by U.S. efforts to extend and defend the liberal international order have provided (and quite unintentionally so) the macroeconomic foundation upon which emerging market governments have built their export-oriented strategies. Large trade surpluses must be offset by large deficits, and U.S. trade deficits have always been largest in the midst of buildup-induced booms. But by providing this foundation, the United States has unintentionally created an international economy in which global prosperity has become dependent on developments in the American economy. As a result, the global imbalances that emerge within this system generate the political dynamics that constitute the greatest threat to the liberal economic order: a nibbling protectionism in the United States as global imbalances develop, more fundamental challenges to the liberal economic order in the wake of financial crises, and political rancor among America's allies and creditors as they battle to distribute the costs of stabilizing the system.

2

National Security Shocks and Military Buildups

> Uncertainty about the meaning of events and especially about prospective threats ... complicates every policy decision. On a good day, you deal with 60-40 odds.
>
> Paul Wolfowitz[1]

What drives changes in U.S. military spending? Answering this question is the critical first step toward a deeper understanding of how the military dimension of American hegemony has shaped postwar economic performance. It is such a critical first step because military spending constitutes one of only a handful of government programs with the ability to impart a powerful stimulus to the American economy. Two simple statistics illustrate this point. First, throughout the postwar period, the defense budget has constituted the largest single category of U.S. federal government discretionary spending. In fiscal year 2012, for instance, the Department of Defense accounted for just over half of total discretionary federal government expenditures. Moreover, the gap between first and second place is huge. The Department of Education received $79.1 billion, roughly 12 percent of the amount allocated to the Department of Defense. Second, because the military accounts for such a large share of the federal budget, it constitutes a substantial share of national expenditures. As a share of total national income, military expenditures have averaged roughly 6 percent across the postwar period. Because military spending occupies so much of federal discretionary spending, and because these

---

[1] Cited in Davis (1996: 37).

expenditures constitute an important share of national income, government decisions about military spending have potential consequences for macroeconomic activity that are unparalleled by any other single private or public activity.

In spite of the economic importance of postwar military spending, we know relatively little about the political dynamics that have driven its variation. This limited insight is not for lack of attention. Research on U.S. defense spending has focused on two models: a threat-driven approach and a bureaucratic politics approach. Throughout the Cold War era, researchers sought to explain U.S. military spending in terms of an arms race between the United States and the Soviet Union (see, e.g., Lambelet 1973; Mintz 1992; Moll and Luebbert 1980; Ostrom and Marra 1986; Richardson 1960). It proved difficult to find systematic evidence that annual changes in American military spending were highly responsive to year-to-year changes in Soviet spending, however. As Cusack and Ward (1981: 448) noted in the early 1980s, this research found "little compelling evidence that an arms race embodies the primary dynamic underlying U.S. defense expenditures" (Cusack and Ward 1981: 448).[2]

Attention shifted to domestic politics, and scholars modeled military spending "as the product of a large, disaggregated, and complex organization where bureaucratic politics and organizational goals and procedures play as important a role ... as the perceived external threat" (Majeski 1989: 130). Some scholars discounted the importance of the external threat even more sharply, seeking to explain military spending as a function of a powerful electoral incentive to manipulate military spending levels to stimulate macroeconomic activity in the run up to national elections (Nincic and Cusack 1979). More recent work explores the impact of ideology on spending levels. Fordham (2007), for instance, examines the impact of partisanship on force composition, and finds that in the U.S. context, Republicans support spending on nuclear weapons while Democrats are more likely to support spending on conventional forces. Whitten and Williams (2011), in a study that excludes the United States, find that ideology interacts with the international security environment to shape military spending. All of this research has made important

---

[2] The imperial overstretch hypothesis is similar to arms race models that postulate a security-maximizing executive who set military spending in response to decisions taken by a rival. Hence, military spending evolves in response to external developments (for an overview of this approach, see Mintz 1992).

contributions, none of it accounts for the central empirical puzzle evident in year-to-year changes of U.S. military spending. The puzzle emerges from the rather peculiar distribution of changes in military spending: the distribution exhibits high peaks and fat tails. That is, most year-to-year changes in military spending are very small: spending in a given fiscal year equals spending in the previous fiscal year plus or minus a small amount. Approximately 66 percent of year-to-year changes in military spending fall into this category. Changes of such magnitude are precisely what one expects to observe in an incremental process dominated by organizational and bureaucratic routines. Occasionally, however, and far more frequently than we would expect if changes in military spending were normally distributed, military spending changes by an extraordinarily large amount. The mean of the eleven largest year-to-year increases is 35 percent. These outcomes are obvious departures from incrementalism. The puzzle, therefore, is: How can a single political process be characterized by the logic of incrementalism most of the time, but generate extremely large changes on more than a few occasions?

War might seem to resolve this puzzle: military expenditures change sharply when the United States fights a war, and change little in other years. Yet, this is a classic begging of the question: it explains the outcome of interest – spending more money on the military – as a function of spending more money on the military (to fight a war). This is especially problematic reasoning for the United States, as in the postwar period the United States has never been forced by foreign invasion to fight a war at home. Instead, American policymakers have been able to choose when, where, and if to participate in wars. These decisions did not occur always under conditions of American choosing, but in every instance American policymakers chose to use military force in an environment in which they could have chosen not to use force without placing the territorial integrity or national sovereignty of the United States at risk. Choice was available even in the wake of the 9/11 attacks. During the 1990s, the Clinton administration relied on the Department of Justice after the first bombing of the Twin Towers and the attack on the USS *Cole*. The Obama administration seems more attached to low-intensity and covert operations. Because U.S. wars have been elective rather than imposed, they are not exogenous events that can be invoked to explain variation in U.S. military spending.

This chapter offers a solution to this puzzle that focuses on the interaction between policymakers' assessments of the international security threat and the institutional characteristics of American politics.

U.S. policymakers have a strong incentive to set military spending in response to the severity of the threat to U.S. interests present in the international system. We expect expenditures to rise as the perceived external threat increases, and when the threat falls, we expect policymakers to cut military spending. Yet, American policymakers cannot know the true threat to American interests present in the system; they can only estimate its severity. Hence, the threat that shapes military spending decisions is more accurately characterized as a distribution of estimates rather than as a point. The mean of this distribution represents the "best estimate" of the threat, while the variance of the distribution represents the uncertainty of the threat estimate – recognition that the threat could be greater or lesser than the best estimate.

The uncertainty that characterizes the threat estimate interacts with institutional characteristics of the American political system to impart a strong status quo bias to military spending most of the time. American political institutions create a multiple veto player system. Some veto points are occupied by doves who believe that the mean threat estimate overstates the true threat. Because they perceive a lesser threat, they accept lower levels of military spending than the level suggested by the mean estimate. Other veto points are occupied by hawks, who believe that the mean threat estimate understates the true threat. Because they perceive a greater threat, they believe military spending should be greater than the level suggested by the mean threat. Because each is a veto player, each blocks the attempts by the other to shift military spending away from the status quo in any direction. Doves veto hawks' efforts to increase military spending, and hawks block doves' efforts to reduce it. Hence, as long as the distribution of the threat estimate is stable, the institutional characteristics of American politics constrain military spending to points close to the status quo.

Large changes in military spending occur only in response to security shocks. Security shocks are unanticipated exogenous events, like the terrorist attacks of September 11, or the collapse of the Berlin Wall and ultimately the Soviet Union itself between October 1989 and December 1991, which alter fundamentally the threat distribution. These shocks provide unambiguous novel information that the security threat is fundamentally greater or lesser than previously believed. Moreover, the clarity of the signal reduces the uncertainty about the threat dramatically. Hence, the mean of the distribution shifts and the variance narrows. As hawks and doves update their beliefs in response to this shock, their preferred military spending levels converge around a budget that is far above (or below) the status quo. As a result, military spending changes sharply.

I develop this argument in three steps. I first articulate the theoretical logic in some detail to derive and defend the core hypotheses. Attention shifts then to empirical evaluation. I demonstrate first that the distribution of spending changes is consistent with a process governed by this logic, highlight the correlation between security shocks and large changes in military spending, and demonstrate that the apparent correlation is robust to other considerations. I then evaluate the causal mechanism. Focusing on the four major military buildups, I draw on primary and secondary sources to demonstrate how the security shock altered the mean and variance of the threat distribution and thus enabled a sharp increase in military spending.

Security Threats, Veto Players, and Changes in Military Spending

In an ideal world, policymakers would set military spending at precisely the level necessary to defend American interests against hostile foreign challenges and they would vary military spending in response to changes in this foreign threat. This idealized logic derives from the recognition that military spending carries costs as well as providing indirect productivity gains (Aizenman and Glick 2006). Opportunity costs arise because employing people and resources to defend the realm makes these resources unavailable for other uses. Indirect productivity gains arise because the security that military power provides increases the incentive to invest, and such investment increases society's capital/labor ratio. Thus, given a constant threat, as military spending increases from zero, marginal benefits initially offset marginal costs. Eventually, however, marginal increases of military power must fail to yield additional benefits (once the realm is secure, additional spending offers no further security), and yet marginal costs remain positive. An omniscient benevolent dictator determined to maximize national welfare, therefore, would set military spending to equate marginal cost and marginal benefit. The level of spending at which these equate will depend on the severity of the threat: marginal benefit equals marginal cost at a higher military force level in a hostile environment than in a relatively peaceful one.

Two factors intervene to push the real world away from this idealized portrait. First, policymakers are not omniscient. In a complex international environment, the threat to American interests is uncertain. The threat to American interests present in the international system is a function of the intentions and the capabilities of foreign actors. Both characteristics are private information: potential foreign rivals have no incentive to reveal either their capabilities or their intentions to American policymakers. Two things follow. First, policymakers have strong incentives to collect and analyze information in order to estimate the threat. One sees evidence of this incentive operating in U.S. policymaking, where the U.S. government spends between $70 and $80 billion each year on intelligence-related activities (Federation of American Scientists 2014). Second, even with such extraordinary effort and resources dedicated to the challenge, policymakers continue to confront considerable uncertainty about the threat they face. Information collected does not generate a single point estimate of the threat. Multiple analysts reviewing the same information reach different conclusions about the threat.

For instance, in the last year of the Ford administration, the Central Intelligence Agency conducted a competitive threat assessment exercise in which individuals outside the established National Intelligence Estimate process developed independent estimates of the Soviet threat from the same information. These so-called team A and team B exercises yielded very different threat estimates. Team B asserted that the information "indicated beyond reasonable doubt that the Soviet leadership ... regarded nuclear weapons as tools of war whose proper employment, in offensive as well as defensive modes, promised victory." In contrast, team A concluded that Soviet leadership's uncertainty about its ability to launch and prevail in a nuclear attack constrained aggressive or reckless behavior (Preble 2005). Consequently, policymakers confront irreducible uncertainty about the threat they face in the international system.

The second factor that pushes military spending away from the stylized ideal is that spending levels are selected through a decision-making process that involves multiple policymakers across multiple departments and branches of the federal government. These multiple veto players typically share the common goal of securing the nation against foreign threats. Almost universally, political elites desire to spend enough on national defense to protect the nation against foreign threats. Yet, in spite of holding this common goal, veto players often hold different preferences over military spending. Some want to spend more, and some want to spend less. Veto players can hold different preferences over the level of military spending because they are drawn from a population that varies along a hawk–dove dimension. Hawks view the world as inherently dangerous and thus tend to prefer more military power. In contrast, doves view the world as less dangerous and believe that potential foreign rivals are willing to cooperate. Distinct outlooks may be a consequence of cognitive processes and holding to different theories of war or they may reflect personality characteristics (Aldrich et al. 2006; D'Agostino 1995; Jervis 1976; Modigliani 1972). Because hawks and doves are typically represented among veto players, military spending decisions typically reflect the outcomes of bargaining between individuals with very different military spending preferences.

We can represent these two central characteristics of the military spending decision making – the uncertainty of the threat and the multiple veto player nature of the decision-making process – with a standard spatial model (Figure 2.1a). The policy dimension represents the amount of military spending, with spending levels rising as we move from left to right. The distribution above the spending dimension represents the distribution of threat estimates generated by the intelligence community. For simplicity, I assume that the threat estimate is the product of an unbiased intelligence gathering process. Although each individual who collects and analyzes intelligence data may be biased, I assume that the distribution of these biases is not itself biased, so that the aggregation of the estimates produced by the many hundreds of individuals involved yields a normal distribution whose mean is an unbiased estimate of the true threat. The intelligence agencies thus generate an estimated threat characterized by the most likely threat level (the mean of the distribution) surrounded by higher and lower estimates (the variance of the distribution).

The location of hawk and dove ideal points along this dimension reflect their threat perceptions relative to the mean threat estimate. Hawks believe that the mean of the threat distribution underestimates the true threat to American interests. Hawks' ideal level of military spending thus positions them somewhere between the distribution's mean and its upper bound. How far from the mean hawks locate depends on how hawkish they are. In Figure 2.1a, the hawk's ideal point (H) sits one standard deviation to the right of the mean. Doves believe that the mean threat estimate likely overestimates the true threat to American interests. They thus position themselves between the mean and the distribution's lower bound. In Figure 2.1a, the dove's ideal point (D) falls one standard deviation to the left of the mean.

Given the environment depicted in Figure 2.1a, military spending will likely be set initially to defend against the mean threat estimate. Because the hawk and the dove each can veto any proposed spending level, it is likely that a series of offers and counter-offers will lead them to the point on the interval midway between their ideal points. Given that the

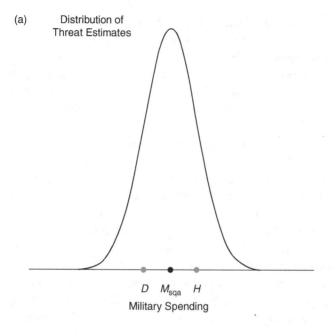

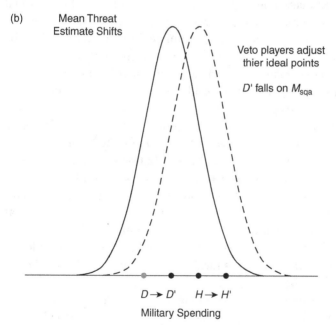

FIGURE 2.1. Security Shocks and the Distribution of Threat Estimates.

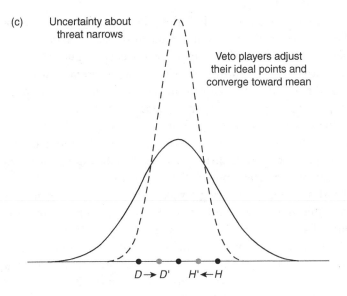

(c) Uncertainty about threat narrows

Veto players adjust their ideal points and converge toward mean

$D \rightarrow D'$ $H' \leftarrow H$

Military Spending

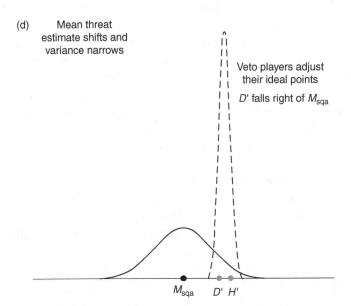

(d) Mean threat estimate shifts and variance narrows

Veto players adjust their ideal points

D' falls right of M_{sqa}

M_{sqa} D' H'

Military Spending

FIGURE 2.1. (*continued*)

two ideal points rest one standard deviation above and below the mean threat, initial military spending lies at the mean threat estimate. Where precisely the status quo lies is less important for current purposes than understanding how the structure of decision making interacts with the distribution of threat estimates to affect movement from any status quo.

Military spending can increase or decrease relative to the status quo only if the distribution of threat estimates changes. The distribution changes in response to new information generated by international events, and veto players update their beliefs of the existing threat based on the new distribution. These new beliefs in turn prompt veto players to alter their ideal military spending levels. New information can alter the threat distribution in three ways. First, new information can alter the mean estimate of the threat to American interests but leave the variance unaffected. Second, new information can reduce the variance of the estimated threat but leave the mean unaffected. Finally, new information can alter the mean and the variance of the threat distribution. Large changes in military spending occur only when the mean threat estimate changes by a large amount and the variance of the distribution narrows substantially. We can understand why by observing how these three changes alter the decision-making environment.

In the first case, a large change in the mean alone is insufficient to generate a large change in spending. Consider the scenario depicted in Figure 2.1b. Here new information has caused a substantial revision of the estimated threat, pushing the mean threat one standard deviation to the right of its initial position. Hawks and doves update their military spending preferences in response to this new information, and reposition themselves one standard above and below this new mean (D' and H'). In this new environment, the hawk is worse off relative to the status quo ante and wants to increase military spending sharply. Doves, however, are better off relative to the status quo ante than before the revised threat estimate, for the inherited military spending (M_{sqa}) falls directly on the new ideal point. Any change in military spending from the status quo therefore reduces doves' utility. As long as the variance remains constant, the mean threat must shift more than one standard deviation to the right of the prior mean for the dove to accept any increase in military spending. Even then, the increase in military spending will be quite small relative to the increased threat estimate.[3] Thus, as long as the distribution of threat

---

[3] Research in cognitive psychology suggests that updating may be more conservative than I characterize it to be here. As Stein (2013: 20) summarizes, "evidence from cognitive

estimates allows hawks and doves to continue to hold very different ideal points, even a large change in the mean estimated threat has little impact on military spending.

In the second case, a large reduction in the variance alone also is insufficient to change in spending. To see why, consider the scenario depicted in Figure 2.1c. As before, spending rests at the mean threat estimate. Now suppose that new information reduces uncertainty about the threat substantially but leaves the mean unaffected. The variance of the distribution narrows and veto players update and adjust their ideal points to remain positioned one standard above and below the mean. The dove recognizes that the world is more threatening and prefers a bit more military spending than previously. The hawk, in contrast, believes the world is less threatening than previously and prefers less spending than he did before the revised threat estimate. Thus, information that merely reduces uncertainty will not generate more military spending; it will simply reduce the degree to which hawks and doves disagree about the ideal level of military spending. For example, such a dynamic possibly characterized the bipartisan American security policy toward the Soviet Union during the pre-Vietnam era. Intelligence allowed for revised estimates of the Soviet threat that reduced the uncertainty that surrounded estimates of the direct military threat to the United States posed by the Soviet Union.

In the third case, when the mean increases or decreases sharply and the variance narrows substantially, military spending increases sharply. This case is depicted in Figure 2.1d. Here the mean threat estimate has shifted one standard deviation to the right: the world is perceived to be much more threatening than prior estimates suggested. Simultaneously, the variance around this mean has narrowed sharply: the new threat estimate is much less uncertain than the previous estimate. The hawk and the dove update their ideal military spending levels in response to this revised threat distribution and reposition themselves one standard deviation above and below the mean. The dove's ideal point is now far to the right of the status quo ante spending level. Consequently, a large increase in military spending provides the dove a substantial utility improvement. The dove thus votes with the hawk to increase military spending.

psychology suggests that these processes are more conservative than rational models suggest, weighed down by prior beliefs and initial estimates. The implications for threat perception are considerable; once an estimate of threat is generated, it anchors subsequent rates of revision so that revision is slower and less responsive to diagnostic information. Threat perceptions consequently become embedded and resistant to change."

Large changes in military spending occur, therefore, in response to events with two distinguishing characteristics. First, the event must demonstrate that the threat is substantially different than the current threat estimate suggests. Events that merely confirm existing estimates, regardless of how substantial a threat they might pose, will not alter the mean. Second, the event must provide unambiguous information; that is, the signal must admit of only a single interpretation in order to reduce the uncertainty surrounding the new threat estimate. In other words, large changes in military spending are likely to occur in response to security shocks: unexpected events that cause all veto players to believe that the level of hostility present in the international system is substantially greater (or lesser) than previously believed and causes the gap between hawks and doves to narrow substantially.

This model offers three observable implications. First, the model offers clear expectations about the distribution of changes in military spending. The distribution of changes in military spending should be leptokurtic: high peaked with heavy or fat tails. That is, most changes in military spending will be quite small, but we will observe a few extremely large changes. Second, the model offers clear expectations about the correlation between changes in the global security environment and changes in military spending. Here we expect changes in military spending to correlate with security shocks. Finally, the model offers expectations regarding the causal mechanism through which security shocks generate large changes in military spending. Security shocks should cause policymakers to update their beliefs about the level of hostility to U.S. interests present in the international system. As a result of this updating, all veto players believe that the threat is substantially greater than they had previously believed, and the difference between hawks and doves should narrow. I turn now to evaluate these expectations.

Military Spending and Security Shocks across Time

I turn first to the distribution of changes in military spending across the postwar period. Recall that the model leads us to expect that the vast majority of changes in military spending will be quite small, and only a few changes will be large. I evaluate these expectations using data on military expenditures compiled by the Policy Agendas Project (True 2009). These data provide a measure of defense spending that is consistent across time. This provides confidence that data for military spending in

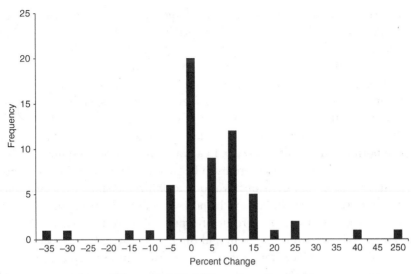

FIGURE 2.2. Annual Change in U.S. Military Spending.

2008 include the same functional purposes as those for 1948. The data also convert current values to constant values, thereby allowing analysts to compare absolute spending levels across time.

Consider first the relative frequency of small and large changes in military expenditures between 1948 and 2008 (Figure 2.2). Notice that defense expenditures increased in real terms in almost half of the post-war years and decreased in real terms in the other half. Not surprisingly, the average increase has been greater than the average reduction; indeed, over the entire sample period the average increase has been twice as large as the average decrease. Second, most changes in defense spending, both increases and decreases, have been quite small. The average change for the full sample is 5.1 percent, but if we remove the seventeen largest changes (positive and negative), the average of the remaining forty-four observations is 0.9 percent.

The seventeen large changes in military spending are extremely large relative to the average change. The thirteen largest increases average 31.5 percent, six times greater than the average of the full sample, and thirty-one times greater than the average of the remaining expenditure increases. These large increases range from 220 percent to 10 percent. Large spending decreases exhibit similar characteristics. The average for the four largest cuts is 23.9 percent (and for the ten largest cuts,

14 percent), and they range from one large cut of 36 percent to a cut of 11 percent. To the naked eye, therefore, the distribution of changes in military spending appears to exhibit high peaks and fat tails.

Statistical measures confirm this impression. The full distribution, including increases and decreases in military spending, is leptokurtic, with a kurtosis statistic of 44.3. If we restrict the sample to spending increases, the distribution remains leptokurtic (kurtosis of 26.7). In addition, the distribution contains far more very large changes than we would expect in a normally distributed sample. In a normally distributed sample of this size, we expect three observations to lie two standard deviations or more from the mean and 0.18 observations to fall three standard deviations or more away from the mean. In postwar military spending, however, seven observations (11.7 percent of total) fall more than two standard deviations away from the mean and three observations (1.85 percent of the sample) fall three standard deviations away from the mean. Even if we restrict the sample to positive increases, large-magnitude increases are far more frequent than a normal distribution expects. Two observations lie more than three standard deviations from the mean, where a normal distribution expects no observations of that magnitude in a sample of this size, and four observations lie further than two standard deviations from the mean against the expected 1.5 such observations in a normal distribution. Our first expectation is thus confirmed: the distribution of changes in military spending is leptokurtic and fat tailed: most changes in military spending are very small, and a few are very large.

This distribution is unlikely to be generated by autonomous developments in domestic politics. A process dominated by bureaucratic politics or constrained by multiple veto players should exhibit incremental growth – small year-to-year changes in spending. And although the resulting distribution of the changes would likely exhibit a high peak, variation would be very compact. That is, the presence of multiple veto players helps us understand why most changes in military spending are small, but offers little insight into why large-magnitude changes occur so frequently. One might hypothesize that these large changes result from developments in presidential politics. Yet, there is little evidence of this. The party of the president is uncorrelated with large increases. About half of these large changes in military spending occur under Democratic administrations (Truman and Johnson); about a quarter fall fully within a Republican term (George W. Bush). The final group of large expenditure increases begins under a Democratic administration and continues during the succeeding Republican administration (Carter to Reagan). Large increases are not related to presidential elections: only one occurs in a presidential election year (Carter in 1980). Finally, the military buildups do not correlate with a change in the president's party: when a Republican succeeds a Democrat in the White House or vice versa. The large increases under Truman and Johnson followed multiple years of Democratic control of the White House. A third series of increases begins under Carter and continues under Reagan. Only in the final group of large increases do we observe a Republican administration succeeding a Democrat and engaging in a military buildup. Presidential politics thus offer no obvious explanation for why a process that typically produces very small changes generates extremely large changes more frequently than we expect.

The large changes in military spending are highly correlated with security shocks. I operationalize security shock as military action by a foreign actor that threatens an important American interest or ally. This definition allows me to identify the set of possible security shocks from the universe of interstate wars that occurred between 1948 and 2002. To minimize complications arising from measuring the novelty of the information these events provide, I assume that each war onset was a surprise for American policymakers. The wars differ, therefore, only in the degree to which they target an American interest or ally.

Twenty-nine interstate wars began in the postwar period (see Table 2.1) (Gleditsch 2004). Five of these conflicts posed large-magnitude security shocks for American policymakers: they involved Soviet clients fighting an American ally (South Korea, South Vietnam), a military invasion that threatened an American interest or ally (Soviet Union invading Afghanistan; Iraq invading Kuwait), or a direct attack on American territory (al Qaeda). Three of these conflicts (the three Arab–Israeli wars) are potential large-magnitude shocks as they involve Soviet clients (Arab states) fighting an American ally (Israel) in an area of vital strategic importance. The remaining twenty-one wars are small-magnitude security shocks; they involved small states fighting over issues with limited significance for American interests.

Four of the five large security shocks are followed by a sequence of very large increases in military spending. This relationship is illustrated in Figure 2.3. North Korea's invasion of South Korea in June of 1950 is followed by three very large military spending increases. The onset of conflict in Vietnam in 1965 is followed by three years in which military spending increases sharply. The Soviet Union's invasion of Afghanistan in 1979 is followed by consecutive large increases in military spending. Finally, the attack on the Twin Towers and the Pentagon on September

TABLE 2.1. *Interstate Wars, 1950–2001*

Conflict	Year War Starts	Year War Ends ———— (If lasts longer than 1 year)	Security Shock	Large Change in U.S. Military Spending
Korean	1950	1953	Yes	Yes
Sino-Tibetan	1950	1951	No	(No)
Russo-Hungarian	1956		No	No
Sinai	1956		No	No
Assam/Sino-Indian	1962		No	No
Vietnamese	1965	1975	Yes	Yes
Second Kashmir	1966		No	No
Six Day	1967		Ambig?	No
Israeli-Egyptian	1969	1970	Ambig?	No
Football	1969		No	No
Bangladesh	1971		No	No
Yom Kippur	1973		Ambig?	No
Turco-Cypriot	1974		No	No
Vietnamese-Cambodian	1975	1979	No	No
Ethiopian-Somalian	1977	1978	No	No
Ugandan-Tanzanian	1978	1979	No	No
Sino-Vietnamese	1979		No	No
Soviet-Afghanistan	1979	1988	Yes	Yes
Iran-Iraq	1980	1988	No	No
Falklands	1982		No	No
Israel-Syria (Lebanon)	1982		No	No
Sino-Vietnamese	1985	1987	No	No
Gulf War	1990	1991	Yes	No
Azeri-Armenian (Nagorno-Karabakh)	1992	1993	No	No
Yugoslavia	1993		No	No
Eritrea-Ethiopia	1998	2000	No	No
India-Pakistani	1999		No	No
NATO-Yugoslavian	1999		No	No
Al-Qaeda-USA	2001	ongoing	Yes	Yes

11, 2001 is followed by a series of large increases. The largest reductions in postwar military spending occur as the United States demobilizes after a war. One large cluster of cuts occurred at the conclusion of the Korean War (1953, 1954, and 1955). A second cluster of large cuts came in the early 1970s as the United States disengaged from Vietnam. The three other largest cuts in military spending (1991, 1993, 1994) are responses

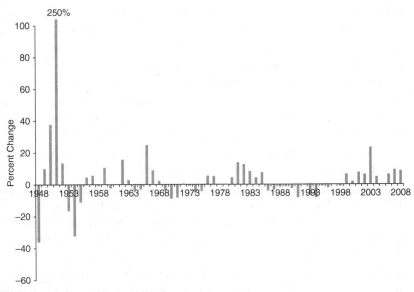

FIGURE 2.3. Security Shocks and Changes in U.S. Military Spending.

to the collapse of the Soviet Union and the consequent end of the Cold War superpower rivalry. One security shock, Iraq's invasion of Kuwait in 1990, did not spark a large military spending increase. This probably reflects the brevity of the conflict (combat operations concluded in about 50 days) and the ability of the United States to secure financial contributions to offset its costs from its allies. Nor did the three Arab–Israeli wars trigger a series of U.S. military buildups. Thus, although not all security shocks triggered a large change in military spending, the vast majority of large changes in military spending were triggered by security shocks.

Notice also that very few large military spending increases occurred without a security shock. Indeed, perhaps this is the most striking finding. One expects military spending to rise sharply in response to the outbreak of a war that targets an important American interest or ally. It is less obvious that such instances would be the only occasions on which U.S. military spending rises sharply. Yet, Figure 2.3 suggests that large military spending increases are exceedingly rare in the absence of foreign military actions that target U.S. interests. The sample contains only two such increases in the late 1950s and early 1960s. Arguably, these constitute partial rather than complete exceptions to the broader pattern, as at least one of these increases occurred in the wake of the *Sputnik* shock, which appeared to suggest that the United States was lagging behind in the space race with potentially dire consequences for U.S. national security. Senator Mike Mansfield is reported to have said in reaction to the *Sputnik* launch, "What is at stake is nothing less than our survival." Lyndon Johnson spoke of an approaching era in which the "Soviets would be dropping bombs on us from space like kids dropping rocks onto cars from freeway overpasses." Other than these two observations, military spending increased by only small amounts in the absence of an external provocation. Thus, large changes in U.S. military spending throughout the postwar period almost never occur as a result of military action that targets an American ally or interest.

To evaluate further the relationships apparent in the descriptive data, I regressed changes in military spending against security shocks while controlling for other factors. The dependent variable is the percent change in military spending presented earlier. I coded the security shocks discussed in Table 2.1 as two-year events from the date they occur.[4] I created a second security shock variable to capture the end of the Cold War; this is also coded as a two-year event. I included presidential election years and the party of the president. In addition, I controlled for changes in Soviet military spending, for unemployment, and for the Cold War and post–Cold War eras. The results are presented in Table 2.2.

The statistical model offers strong support for the core argument. Security shocks account for a substantial portion of the variation in postwar changes in military spending. Positive security shocks have been associated with military expenditure increases of almost 20 percent on average. The negative shock of the end of the Cold War was associated with a cut in military spending of about equal magnitude. In addition, changes in military spending exhibit positive feedback, as change in $t - 1$ is positively associated with change in year t. Thus, spending is highly responsive to global security shocks, and these shocks have a persistent impact on spending changes.

None of the other variables appear to have any systematic relationship with changes in military spending. Changes in Soviet military spending are signed correctly, but do not approach traditional levels of statistical significance. This result does not change even when one conditions the

[4] I ran the model with security shock coded two different ways – a one-year impact and the reported two-year impact. None of the results change substantially across the two models. None of the variables that are significant cease to be significant; none of the variables that are not significant in this specification become significant in the model that relies on the alternative coding. However, overall model fit is somewhat better with the two-year window.

TABLE 2.2. *Security Shocks and Changes in Military Spending, 1948–2008*

	Changes in Military Spending	Log of Absolute Value	Log of Positive Changes
Security Shock	19.83	0.56	1.28
	(3.84)	(0.16)	(0.51)
Change in Military Spending$_{t-1}$	0.43	0.49	0.09
	(0.10)	(0.11)	(0.18)
Soviet Spending$_{t-1}$	0.38	−6.75e-10	1.30
	(3.75)	(7.99e-10)	(1.59)
Unemployment$_{t-1}$	−2.66	0.03	−0.10
	(1.36)	(0.06)	(0.16)
Presidential Election Year	−3.3	−0.31	−0.68
	(3.07)	(0.18)	(0.54)
Party of the President	−0.87	−0.08	−0.21
	(2.98)	(0.14)	(0.65)
End of Cold War	−22.17	−0.61	
	(8.24)	(0.38)	
Constant	0.44	0.33	2.90
	(1.97)	(0.15)	(0.96)
Rho	0.004	−0.32	
Observations	59	59	30
Adjusted R^2	0.49	0.40	0.28
F Statistic	8.93	5.96	2.10

impact of Soviet spending on the Cold War by including an interaction term in the model. Change in unemployment is significantly related to changes in military spending, but the relationship is negative rather than positive, suggesting that increases in military spending are much smaller during recessions than during booms. The model offers no indication that changes in military spending are larger during presidential election years than in other years, or that such spending varies systematically with the party of the president.

Because the dependent variable is not normally distributed, I re-estimated the model after normalizing changes in military spending. To normalize changes in military spending I transformed the raw data into the log of the absolute values. The results from this model are presented in column 2 of Table 2.2. Notice that although the magnitude of the coefficients changes, the statistical significance does not. Of particular importance, the index of security shocks retains statistical significance. Moreover, the coefficient on the security shock variable indicates that a shock in year t increases the change in military spending by approximately 56 percent. As a final robustness check, I estimated the same model against a sample that includes only the positive increases in military spending. This reduces the sample by half to thirty observations. Nevertheless, security shock continues to return a large positive coefficient – indeed the estimated effect doubles in magnitude, suggesting that the average change in the year of a security shock is more than 100 percent larger than the increase in non-shock years – that is statistically significant. The other variables continue to return coefficients that fail to approach conventional levels of statistical significance.

Overall, then, there appears to be substantial evidence that the evolution of postwar military spending has been shaped by the interaction between institutional constraints and exogenous security shocks. Large changes in military spending have occurred in response to security shocks. We rarely observe large increases occurring in the absence of security shocks, and we find little evidence that other characteristics of domestic politics account for the large sudden increases.

Evaluating the Causal Mechanism

Our final step is to evaluate the causal mechanism through which security shocks spark large changes in military spending. The theoretical model suggested that decisions about military spending typically are constrained by disagreement between hawks and doves in an environment characterized by uncertainty about the threat to American interests. Security shocks increase (or decrease) the mean threat estimate and reduce the variance around this mean. As hawks and doves update their beliefs in response to this change in the distribution, their ideal spending levels shift. In particular, doves become willing to support larger military spending because of the shock than they had been willing to accept prior to the shock. I evaluate this expectation by examining the impact of security shocks on the decision-making environment in the four episodes identified above.

We look first at the Korean War. The decision-making environment in this episode is depicted in Figure 2.4. By the spring of 1950 American policymakers generally agreed that the Soviet Union posed a serious threat to American interests and allies. Moreover, the mean estimate of the Soviet threat had risen fairly sharply over the previous year. Yet, considerable uncertainty remained as to whether the Soviets constituted a military threat that required a large and sustained American

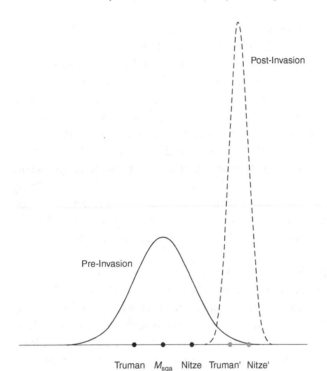

FIGURE 2.4. Korea, 1949–1950.

military buildup. A group of hawks, led by Paul Nitze, believed that the Soviets represented a powerful military threat. These hawks interpreted the information revealed by Soviet atomic weapons tests and Soviet assertiveness in Central Europe as evidence of Soviet willingness to risk military confrontation with the United States in order to achieve their objectives. As Nitze wrote in February 1950, "recent Soviet moves reflect not only a mounting militancy but suggest a boldness that is essentially new – and borders on recklessness … Nothing about the moves indicate that Moscow is preparing to launch in the near future an all-out military attack on the West. They do, however, suggest a greater willingness than in the past to undertake a course of action, including a possible use of force in local areas, which might lead to an accidental outbreak of general military conflict" (Pollard 1989: 228–229). Nitze assembled the hawks into a coherent coalition that put together NSC-68, a document that advanced a very hawkish view of the Soviet threat and called for a substantial increase of U.S. military spending in response.

This relatively hawkish assessment of the Soviet threat was not held universally within the administration. The hawk view sat next to a "widely shared conviction that the Soviets would probably not launch a general war in the near future and that burdensome military expenditures were not a cost effective way to meet the Soviet threat" (Pollard 1989: 219). George Kennan, a leading voice in dove faction, argued as late as the spring of 1950, "That there is little justification for the impression" advanced by the hawks, that the Cold War had suddenly taken a turn to the disadvantage of the United States. The thrust of the Soviet challenge remained ideological and societal/political rather than military (Brune 1989; Wells 1979: 128). Others shared Kennan's relatively dovish orientation, including Charles Bohlen in the State Department, who saw a moderate military threat in the Soviet Union, and Truman himself, who was seeking to constrain military spending to $15 billion.

Given the gap between the hawks and the doves allowed by existing uncertainty about the estimated Soviet threat, determined efforts by the hawks to increase military spending was effectively blocked by administration doves, who saw no benefit from such an increase. Indeed, Truman's immediate response to NSC-68, when he saw it in draft form in the spring of 1950, was to create an ad hoc committee to evaluate the cost of the military buildup Nitze's group proposed (Wells 1979: 137).

And even had the administration unified around the hawk position, its members would have confronted substantial challenges in Congress. The Nationalist Republicans, led by Robert Taft (R-OH) and Kenneth Wherry (R-NE), that constituted a significant block in 1950 were skeptical of the magnitude of the Soviet threat and were quite unwilling to countenance large military budgets. Wherry expressed hope in early 1950 for a negotiated agreement with the Soviet Union that would enable the United States to "put its financial house in order, reduce taxes, and keep off our backs controls, regimentations, and directives issued by our federal bureaus" (Fordham 1998: 112). Taft, who moved increasingly to the front of the Republican Party on foreign policy issues as Arthur Vandenburg fell ill, was deeply skeptical of the expanse of the commitments the United States had embraced (Berger 1975). In the face of this opposition, getting new military spending plans through Congress was a major challenge.

North Korea's invasion of South Korea altered the mean and the variance of the distribution of threat estimates. President Truman communicated his updated beliefs to the congressional leadership in White House meetings and to a joint session of Congress in the following terms: the invasion demonstrated that the communist world had "passed beyond the use of subversion ... to the use of armed invasion and war" (Gaddis 1982: 110). There was no disagreement about the extent of Soviet involvement or the severity of the threat to American interests. As a State Department analysis concluded: this "move against South Korea must be considered a Soviet move" that threatened the credibility and will of the US to defend Japan, Southeast Asia, and Europe (Bernstein 1989: 420). It became widely believed that action in Korea struck directly at American interests. As Truman articulated to the congressional leadership in a White House meeting on June 27th: "If we let Korea down, the Soviets will keep right on going and swallow up one piece of Asia after another ... If we were to let Asia go, the Near East would collapse and no telling what would happen in Europe" (Bernstein 1989: 423).

As uncertainty about the Soviet military threat narrowed, administration doves' ideal military spending levels rose sharply above current spending levels. As they did, military spending levels rose sharply as well. The Truman administration quickly submitted two supplemental appropriations bills to Congress to pay for U.S. involvement in Korea and to enhance U.S. military capabilities more generally. The first, submitted in late July, requested an additional $11 billion. The second, submitted late in 1950, sought an additional $17 billion. These supplemental appropriations were followed by two smaller requests in the first half of 1951. Military spending thus rose by 38 percent in 1950 and by 220 percent in 1951 as U.S. forces moved into Korea. Both houses of Congress approved these supplemental appropriations by large majorities.

The second set of large increases of military spending occurred as the United States escalated its involvement in Vietnam. This episode differs from the Korean conflict in one important way – it lacked a single massive security shock like North Korea's invasion. Nevertheless, the Vietnam escalation exhibits a similar process in which decisions are driven by information provided by security shocks that alter the distribution of threat estimates. The decision-making environment in 1964–1965 is depicted in Figure 2.5. Through 1964, estimates of the threat to American interests posed by the situation in Vietnam allowed doves and hawks to hold widely divergent ideal military spending levels. Secretary of Defense Robert McNamara and Johnson's national security advisor, McGeorge Bundy, were the most vocal hawks in the administration. The dove position, advanced most forcefully by Under Secretary of State George Ball, argued against deepening U.S. military involvement and pressed for a negotiated settlement. This hawk–dove divide within the administration was echoed in Congress, where some congressional leaders (such

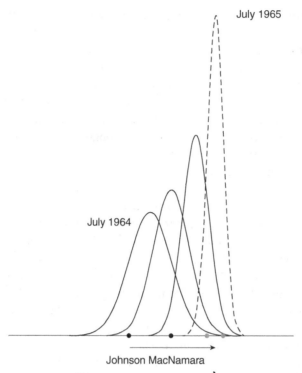

FIGURE 2.5. Vietnam, 1964–1965.

as Mike Mansfield and J. William Fulbright) saw few U.S. interests at stake in Vietnam and argued strongly against an escalation of U.S. military involvement while others, including Richard Russell and many other Southern congressmen, saw the Soviet hand at play and supported an increased military role for the American military forces. Doves located themselves at the left of the threat distribution, while hawks were far to the right.

Given the uncertainty about the severity of the threat and the consequent gap between veto player positions, decision-making dynamics through mid-1964 revolved around hawks pushing for deeper U.S. involvement and doves resisting. Because doves could veto movement from the status quo, U.S. policy remained unchanged. The administration's review of policy, concluded in early 1964, advocated adherence to status quo: the United States would not increase personnel or resources in the region, but the United States would not withdraw support from the regime either (Secretary of Defense 1964a, 1964b).

Escalation followed a series of military actions by the Vietcong against U.S. military targets in South Vietnam during 1964 and early 1965 that altered estimates of the threat North Vietnam posed to U.S. interests and narrowed the variance of the distribution. In contrast to the Korean War, no single security shock was decisive in bringing about this change in the evaluation of the situation. Instead, the cumulative impact of a series of events altered the distribution. As Johnson summarized in his memoirs, "the decision [to escalate US involvement in 1965] was made because it had become clear, gradually but unmistakably, that Hanoi was moving in for the kill" (Johnson 1971: 132). The series of events that made the threat more certain began with the Gulf of Tonkin incidents of August 1964. Gulf of Tonkin was followed by a series of attacks on U.S. targets in South Vietnam, culminating in the raid on Pleiku air base in early February 1965. By early 1965, the revised threat estimate held that the South Vietnamese regime could not survive given the current level of U.S. involvement. McGeorge Bundy summarized the situation for Johnson in February 1965: "The situation in Vietnam is deteriorating, and without new U.S. action defeat appears inevitable – probably not in a matter of weeks or perhaps even months, but within the next year or so" (Bundy 1965).

As the distribution of threat estimates changed, veto players updated their beliefs and repositioned themselves along the military spending dimension. Johnson was the critical veto player. As he became convinced that the situation was deteriorating, he became more willing to escalate U.S. involvement. Thus the gap between hawks and doves in the White House narrowed. The narrowing gap extended to the congressional leadership as well. Records of White House meetings between Johnson and the congressional leadership between August 1964 and July 1965 indicate how little disagreement there was about the situation the United States confronted in Vietnam. The congressional leadership raised no concerns about regime survival during a White House meeting in the summer of 1964 (Executive Office of the President 1964). Congressional concern began to rise in early 1965, and by July appears to have converged on the belief that South Vietnam's survival as an independent state was in jeopardy (Executive Office of the President 1965a, 1965b).

The variance of the distribution narrowed less in this case than it did following North Korea's invasion in June 1950. Critics of the administration's decisions were present and the most prominent of them – including Fulbright and Mansfield – made their disagreement known to Johnson. George Ball remained opposed to escalation, in part because he believed that an American withdrawal would be less damaging to American interests, an assessment that differed sharply from the hawk position. Indeed, administration hawks appear to have been keenly aware that absent shocks such as those that occurred between June 1964 and July 1965, Congress would be unlikely to support deeper U.S. involvement. Meeting on June 10, 1964 administration officials agreed that Congress was unlikely to support administration requests when, as Dean Rusk summarized, "circumstances are such as to require action, and, thereby, force congressional action" (Gibbons 1994: 11–12). Arguably, administration hardliners enacted this strategy, taking advantage of events as they occurred in Vietnam to first gain Johnson's assent and then congressional support for increased U.S. involvement in Vietnam. But, the possibility that officials acted opportunistically and used security shocks to loosen the constraints they faced doesn't undermine the broader point: in the absence of these security shocks, the constraints would not be easily escaped.

The third episode differs from these two prior cases in two ways. First, in this case the security shock came from direct Soviet military action – the Soviet invasion of Afghanistan – rather than from the activities of a Soviet client. Second, the U.S. response did not include military action against a hostile force, but was limited to a sustained military buildup. The decision-making environment for this episode is illustrated in Figure 2.6. Carter's presidency was characterized by a wide gap between hawk and dove preferences over military spending that reflected radically different evaluations of the Soviet military threat. Carter was the leading dove. He was relatively sanguine about the military dimension of the Soviet challenge. As Skidmore (1996: 38) summarizes, President Carter "respected Soviet military might and viewed increases in Soviet activities in the Third World as challenging." He "did not, however, perceive broad geopolitical designs in Soviet behavior." Indeed, Carter believed that he could treat developments in the developing world independent of East–West relationships. And he believed that he could use the détente process and arms control negotiations to promote a more cooperative relationship with the Soviet Union.

Although Carter and many of his foreign policy team were relatively dovish regarding the Soviet Union, the administration also contained many anti-Soviet hawks. His National Security Advisor, Zbigniew Brzezinski, was the most influential. Congress contained additional prominent anti-Soviet democratic hawks (Henry "Scoop" Jackson in particular). Influential private groups (such as the Committee on the Present Danger) were continually stressing the severity of the Soviet military

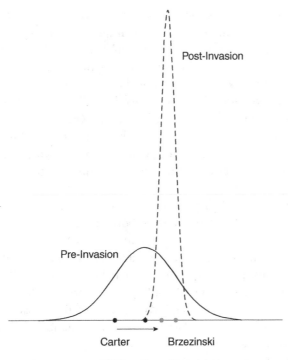

FIGURE 2.6. Afghanistan, 1978–1980.

challenge. These voices asserted that the Soviet Union remained determined to extend its influence at American expense, was willing to use military power to do so, and that the only way to check Soviet expansion was to strengthen American military power substantially.

Carter thus positioned himself below the mean of the distribution of threat estimate and saw no benefit from increased military expenditures. Brzezinski and the hawks in Congress and in the wings positioned themselves well to the right of the mean and pressed hard for increased military spending. Yet, given Carter's ideal point, the best that hawks could achieve was to constrain Carter's ability to reduce military spending still further. As a result, the administration proposed very modest nominal increases in military expenditures for fiscal years 1978 and 1979. Indeed, given the high inflation of the period, real defense expenditures fell in these two years.

The Soviet invasion of Afghanistan in December 1979 raised the mean and reduced the variance of the distribution of threat estimates. The central concern that the Soviet invasion sparked was continued access to Persian Gulf oil. "Oil is the lifeblood of modem industrial societies," Secretary of Defense Harold Brown proclaimed in March 1980. "The loss of this oil ... would be a blow of catastrophic proportions ... Soviet control of this area would make economic vassals of much of both the industrialized and the less developed worlds" (cited in Leffler 1983: 246). The possibility of Soviet control of the flow of oil to the West was accentuated by the recent experience of the Arab oil embargo of 1973 and the second oil shock that occurred in connection with the Iranian revolution. These energy price shocks had powerful negative consequences for economic performance in the United States.

President Carter revised his beliefs about the military threat posed by the Soviet Union rather fundamentally in response to this new information. Although administration officials kept an eye on Soviet activities around Afghanistan through 1979, it is generally conceded that the intelligence community greatly underestimated the likelihood of a Soviet invasion of Afghanistan (Diamond 2008: 73). As Carter explained to a journalist shortly after the invasion, "My opinion of the Russians has changed most dramatically in the last week ... [T]his action of the Soviets has made a more dramatic change in my own opinion of what the Soviets' ultimate goals are than anything they've done in the previous time I've been in office" (see also Aronoff 2006; Smith 1986: 223–224). The direction of the change was equally clear: Carter came to believe that the Soviet leadership was willing to use military force to advance its goals unless the United States demonstrated its determination to resist. As Glad (2009: 205) summarized, "after the Afghan intervention, Carter fully accepted the Brzezinski line that to not stand up to the USSR would simply wet the Soviet appetite." According to this view, world peace since World War II had rested on U.S. determination to resist Soviet probes in the Far East and Europe. The Soviet invasion suggested that the United States must extend this effort into the Near East. "We are, if you will, in the third phase of the great architectural response that the United States launched in the wake of World War II" (Glad 2009: 205).

The administration altered military spending sharply in response. Carter became determined to punish the Soviets for the invasion, and sought "to make sure that Afghanistan will be their Vietnam." Carter increased U.S. funding for the mujahedeen and enunciated the so-called Carter Doctrine in his 1980 State of the Union address. Carter threw his support to the hawks in his administration and in Congress and agreed to increase U.S. military spending substantially. As a first step, he proposed

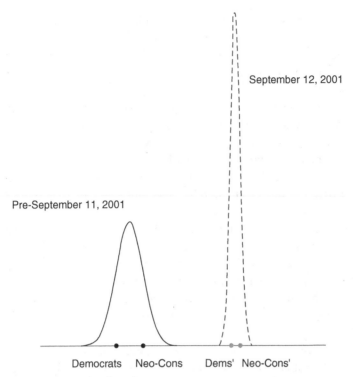

FIGURE 2.7. 9/11 Attack, 2000–2001.

to increase defense spending by 5.4 percent in real terms in 1980 and by 25 percent over a five-year period. Once again, a security shock transformed disagreement among veto players that constrained military spending into a broad consensus that enabled military expenditures to increase sharply.

The final episode, which was triggered by the terrorist attacks of September 11, 2001, differs in one fundamental way from the first three. It is the only postwar instance of a military attack on the American homeland. The decision-making environment for this final episode is depicted by Figure 2.7. In contrast to the three Cold War cases where the mean threat estimate was relatively high and ideal spending levels of hawks and doves were far apart, the pre-9/11 environment combined a relatively low mean threat estimate and a rather compact variance. In the first post–Cold War decade, the typical American national security official saw no major security challenge in the international system. Indeed, the Clinton administration's final National Security Strategy, published in

2000, began as follows: "As we enter the new millennium, we are blessed to be citizens of a country enjoying record prosperity, with no deep divisions at home, *no overriding external threats abroad*, and history's most powerful military ready to defend our interests around the world" (The White House 2000: iii).

Though some policymakers were concerned about the terrorist threat, there was no widely held belief that Islamic extremists were capable of launching a large attack on American soil. As the authoritative 9–11 Commission concluded, "both Presidents Bill Clinton and George Bush and their top advisers told us they got the picture – they understood Bin Ladin was a danger. But given the character and pace of their policy efforts, we do not believe they fully understood just how many people al Qaeda might kill, and how soon it might do it. At some level that is hard to define, we believe the threat had not yet become compelling" (9–11 Commission 2004: 342–343). The Commission criticized Congress for a similar failure to appreciate the threat in the pre-9/11 environment. "The legislative branch adjusted little and did not restructure itself to address changing threats. Its attention to terrorism was episodic and splintered" (Ibid: 107).

The familiar hawk–dove divide was present, but quite compact. Some congressional Republicans pushed for higher military spending (Dao 2001b). Kagan and Kristol summarized this conservative point of view in an editorial in the *Weekly Standard*, in which they asserted that President Bush risked going down in history as the president who allowed U.S. military power to atrophy (Kagan and Kristol 2001). Other Republicans, as well as many Congressional Democrats, argued that increased military spending was not urgent; "this is not a terribly hawkish world" noted James Pinkerton (Dao 2001a: A18). Thus, whereas hawks wanted to increase spending moderately, doves wanted to hold the line.

In this low threat estimate environment, defense spending took a back seat to other policy concerns. Newly elected President George W. Bush declared education his top priority in his first State of the Union address, and rather than increase military spending he asked Secretary of Defense Donald Rumsfeld to conduct an extensive review of force structure and make recommendations for reorganization. In the spring of 2001, the White House proposed increasing defense outlays by $14 billion in 2002 and $9 billion in 2003 (Executive Office of the President of the United States 2001: 19). In this environment, there was little pressure for large increases in military spending and little chance of getting one through Congress given the doves' threat assessment (Towell 2001).

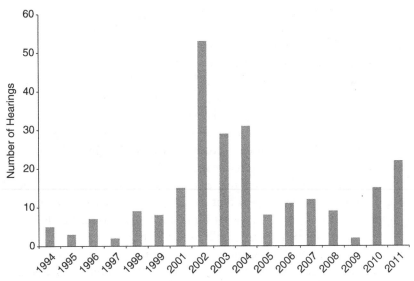

FIGURE 2.8. Attention Dedicated to Terrorism 1993–2011.

The September 11 attack altered the mean threat estimate quite sharply and further reduced the variance. Evidence of the shift in beliefs about the threat posed by terrorist groups lies in the amount of high-level attention Congress and the executive dedicated to terrorism in the years surrounding the attack (Figure 2.8). The measure of congressional attention is the number of House and Senate Hearings dedicated to terrorism occurred in each year. The measure of executive attention is the number of times terrorism is mentioned in the State of the Union address. All three series track the same trend; terrorism received very little attention in Congress and received little attention in the State of the Union address until the 2001 attack. In the immediate aftermath of the attack, the House, the Senate, and the executive branch dedicated substantial attention to the threat to American interests posed by global terrorist networks.

Not only did terrorism receive more attention, but there was also little disagreement that it constituted a serious threat. This compact distribution is evident in the overwhelming congressional support for the use of military power against terrorists and those who harbored them. The House passed the Authorization for Use of Military Force Against Terrorists on September 14, 2001 by a vote of 420 to 1 (with 10 not voting). The Senate passed the bill by a vote of 98 to 0, with two senators present but not voting. Shortly thereafter, the House approved a $343 billion defense budget by a 398 to 17 majority, and the Senate followed by passing a slightly larger bill by a 99 to 0 majority. This broad consensus persisted, though less firmly, through the vote on the Authorization for use of Military Force Against Iraq in October 2002. This bill passed in the House and Senate with smaller, but still overwhelming majorities: 297 to 133 in the House and 77 to 23 in the Senate.

We therefore see broadly similar causal mechanisms in all four episodes. In the pre-shock environment, uncertainty about the international threat allowed hawks and doves to hold widely divergent ideal military spending levels. Hawks invariably argued that the mean underestimated the threat and advocated for higher than the status quo military spending. Doves invariably argued that the threat was well below the mean estimate, and sought to reduce spending. In this environment, changes in military spending were quite small. Security shocks altered the variance and the mean of the threat estimate distribution. In particular, these unexpected military actions that targeted important U.S. interests caused policymakers to greatly increase the estimated threat and to sharply reduce the uncertainty around this estimate. As doves updated their beliefs in response to this new threat estimate, they increased their ideal military spending levels quite substantially.

Conclusion

We began this chapter with a simple question: What has driven changes in postwar US military spending? As we noted, the distribution of changes in military spending is leptokurtic, characterized by tall peaks and fat tails. This means that most year-to-year changes in postwar military spending have been very small, but a few, and far more than we expect, have been quite large. What are the characteristics of the political process that seem to powerfully constrain military spending most of the time, but permit very large changes to these expenditures on occasion?

This chapter offered an answer to this question based on the interaction between estimates of the international security threat and institutional characteristics of American politics. I have argued that American policymakers have varied military spending in response to the severity of the threat to U.S. interests present in the international system. Their ability to vary military spending in response to this threat is constrained by two factors. First, American policymakers do not know the true threat to American interests present in the system. The threat estimate is better characterized as a distribution rather than as a point. The mean of this distribution represents the "best estimate" of the threat, while the variance of the distribution represents the uncertainty of the threat estimate – recognition that the threat could be greater or lesser than the best estimate.

Second, the uncertainty that surrounds the threat estimate interacts with institutional characteristics of the American political system to impart a strong status quo bias to military spending. In every postwar administration, hawks and doves positioned themselves at different points under the distribution of threat estimates. Doves believed that the mean threat estimate overstated the true threat and preferred correspondingly lower levels of military spending. Hawks believed that the mean threat estimate understated the true threat and preferred correspondingly higher levels of military spending. Once spending is set, each blocks subsequent efforts by the other to pull military spending closer to their ideal point. Consequently, most changes in military spending are quite small.

The system produces large changes in military spending in response to global security shocks. Global security shocks are fully unanticipated exogenous events, such as the terrorist attacks of September 11, the collapse of the Soviet Bloc, and the Soviet invasion of Afghanistan, which alter fundamentally the distribution of threat estimates. These shocks provided unambiguous novel information that the security threat is much greater or lesser than previously believed. Moreover, the clarity of the signal reduced the uncertainty around this threat substantially. Hence, the mean of the threat estimate distribution shifts and the variance narrows. As hawks and doves update their beliefs in response to this shock, their preferred military spending levels converge around a budget that is far above (or below) the status quo. As a result, military spending changes sharply.

3

Warfare, Welfare, and the Size of the American State

> The problem with government is that government can't say, 'yes' ... There are fifteen or twenty people who have to agree.
>
> James Q. Wilson[1]

Budget politics since 1965, with perhaps a brief reprieve during the mid-1970s, have been dominated by efforts to rein in budget deficits. The federal government has recorded deficits in just about every year of this almost half century, managing to keep expenditures below revenues only in 1969 and then forty years later in 1998–2001. Across this period, postwar budget deficits averaged 2.6 percent of gross domestic product (GDP), climbing to as large as 6 percent of GDP during the 1980s. In spite of the apparent permanence of budget deficits, American politicians have refused to embrace them as an ordinary element of America's post-war political economy. Instead, deficit reduction has become the focus of intense bargaining between key players in the executive branch and Congress. Efforts to reduce deficits usually entail negotiating agreements that provide some combination of higher taxes and reduced spending on social welfare programs.

Although large cuts to military spending have rarely occupied a prominent role in the deficit reduction negotiations, military buildups have nevertheless pushed deficit reduction to the fore of American budget politics for two reasons. First, postwar military buildups have created the large and persistent budget imbalances that generate the pressure for

---

[1] Wilson (1991: 317).

deficit reduction in the first place. Second, the nature of the security shock that sparks the increase in military spending that generates the budget imbalance means that the single largest discretionary spending program is removed from the set of programs that can be adjusted to reduce the budget deficit. Thus, military buildups undertaken in response to security shocks have forced policymakers to reduce a large deficit by negotiating mutually acceptable packages of higher taxes and reduced social welfare spending.

The ability of the administration and Congress to agree on deficit reduction packages has been delayed by many years in every instance since 1960. Delay has been the consequence of the need for executive branch officials and congressional leadership to agree on one of many possible deficit reduction packages. There are multiple paths to deficit reduction. Most simply, policymakers may enact temporary spending reductions in social welfare programs or they may adopt measures that increase tax revenue. And with the exception of the summer of 1950, executive branch officials and key members of Congress have had very different preferences over these alternative adjustment paths. When the executive branch wanted additional revenue, congressional leaders wanted expenditure reductions. When congressional leaders wanted higher taxes, the administration sought cuts to social programs. Disagreement over how to adjust, even when all parties want to adjust, has delayed adoption of deficit reduction measures.

The institutional characteristics of the American political system further amplify this political conflict by transforming adjustment of a budget imbalance generated by a temporary increase of military spending in response to a security emergency into a fundamental struggle over the appropriate size and role of the state in the American economy. This transformation occurs because although the deficit is temporary, each veto player recognizes that given the status quo bias of the American political system, any adjustment package adopted today will have persistent consequences. Temporary tax increases will persist as advocates of an expanded state role in the economy divert the revenues they generate to the expansion of nonmilitary programs once the military conflict that produced them initially ends. Temporary reductions of social welfare spending become persistent as opponents of a larger role for the state in the economy block legislation that would restore social funding to pre-conflict levels. The battle over how to adjust the budget in response to a temporary emergency is thus transformed into a deeper struggle over the size and role of the state in the American economy.

The chapter develops this argument in two stages. I first document the impact that military buildups have had on the federal budget since World War II. I demonstrate that the three military buildups since 1960 have generated large and persistent budget deficits, whereas the Korean War buildup produced a small budget surplus. I then suggest that budget deficits generated by these postwar military buildups have been the largest and most persistent that the United States has experienced since World War II. I then explain why buildups since the Korean conflict have generated deficits, whereas the Korean War buildup did not. The argument I develop focuses on the homogeneity of veto players' preferences over tax increases and expenditure cuts. In 1950 and 1951 policymakers agreed on how to adjust the budget and thus quickly enacted the necessary legislation. Ever since the mid-1960s, however, veto players have disagreed sharply over how to accommodate the larger military expenditures they all agreed were necessary. These disagreements quickly devolved into conflict over the appropriate role for the state in the American economy.

Military Buildups and the Federal Budget

Military buildups have generally, but not always, generated large and persistent budget deficits. The impact of these additional military expenditures on the budget balance is clearly evident in Figure 3.1, which traces the evolution of the federal budget balance as a share of GDP in the years following the start of the military buildup. In three of the four cases, the federal government budget moves sharply into deficit as the buildup begins, with a deterioration of between two and three percent of GDP. And in each episode, the enlarged budget deficit persists for multiple years. In two instances, more than three years elapse before the budget returns to its pre-security shock position. In the third episode, the budget still has not returned to its pre-buildup balance seven years following the initial shock. Although buildups typically have generated large and persistent deficits, they haven't always done so. The Korean War military buildup stands out as a clear exception to the broader pattern; the budget moves from small deficit in the onset year to a large surplus as the war-related buildup begins. The budget remains in surplus until the conflict ends.

These military buildups had a much larger sudden impact on government spending than did other programs initiated during the period. For instance, the National Aeronautic and Space Agency (NASA), which was established in the summer of 1958, saw its budget rise to 4.4 percent of

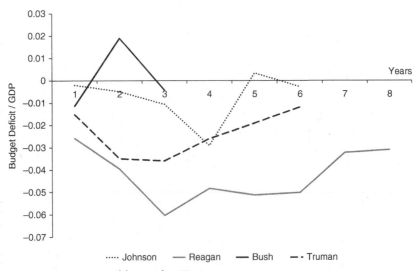

FIGURE 3.1. Post-Buildup Budget Trajectory.

federal government expenditures between 1958 and 1966, an amount equal to about 0.9 percent of current GDP or half the size of the typical military buildup. Moreover, NASA's budget rose slowly during this period, capturing 1 percent more of federal spending each year between 1963 and 1966. Or consider the immediate impact of Medicare in the mid-1960s. Federal spending on healthcare rose from 0.5 percent of GDP to 1 percent of GDP between 1965 and 1967, but this increased spending on healthcare was funded by an increase of the payroll tax (FICA). The impact of Medicare Part D is also relatively small. Though this law was passed in 2003, it was not implemented until January 1, 2006. In 2008, federal expenditures in the program totaled $49.3 billion, approximately 0.03 percent of GDP. Indeed, only three postwar expenditures rival the magnitude of military buildups – the 1970 capitalization of the U.S. Postal Service, the 1978 funding of the strategic oil reserve, and the 2005 disaster relief enacted in the wake of Hurricane Katrina. Thus, military buildups have had a distinctive impact on the budget across the postwar period.

Not only have military buildups generated budget deficits, but the deficits they have created also have been the largest and most persistent that the United States has run in the postwar era. As Figure 3.2 highlights, the federal budget has deteriorated on nine occasions since 1950. In six instances, the budget deteriorated as a slide into recession caused

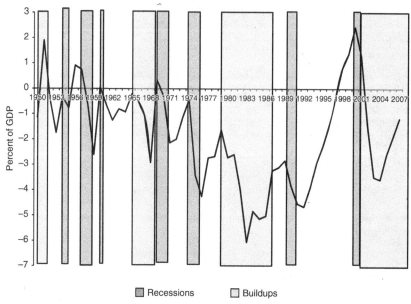

FIGURE 3.2. Military Buildups, Recessions, and Budget Deficits.

tax revenues to fall and automatic stabilizer expenditures to rise. These deficits were relatively small – a worsening of around 1 percent of GDP on average – short lived, and typically not a result of intentional policy shifts. The budget balance improved substantially as the economy recovered, and in almost every instance recessions lasted one year or less. On three occasions, however, the budget deterioration occurred as the United States ramped up military spending in response to a security shock. These budget deficits have been twice as large as deficits resulting from recessions and they have persisted far into the recovery phase of the business cycle. The other postwar budget shocks occurred as a reaction to natural disasters (Hurricane Katrina) and banking crises in 1989 and 2008. Thus, military buildups seem to represent the only policy choice that repeatedly has had a large negative impact on the budget balance.

Of course, the budgetary consequence of legislated tax cuts is a potentially confounding factor. Quite serendipitously, the three largest postwar tax rate reductions have occurred very close in time to the three post–Korean War military buildups. Two of these major tax cuts, those enacted in 1964 by the Kennedy–Johnson administration and in 2001 by the Bush administration, preceded the security shocks that sparked the military buildup by about one year. The third major tax cut, enacted by the Reagan administration in 1981, followed the decision to increase military spending in response to the Soviet invasion of Afghanistan by slightly more than a year. The estimated impact of each reduction in tax rates was to reduce revenue by between 1 and 2 percent of GDP, though these reductions were implemented over a multiyear timeframe (Romer and Romer 2008). The deficits that we see emerge as the military build-ups begin might thus reflect the impact of the tax rate reduction as well as the impact of the additional military expenditures.

We can evaluate more systematically the impact of military build-ups, tax legislation, and other economic and political factors on the budget deficit with a time series model. The time series model regresses the year-to-year change in the budget balance as a percent of GDP against *Changes in Military Spending*, the three major tax bills, and a set of control variables. The dependent variable is the one-year change in the budget balance. The percent change in military spending is the key independent variable. To capture the impact of the three tax acts I created a dichotomous variable for each act. These variables take the value zero in all years through the year the act was passed, and the value one in all subsequent years. To capture electoral and partisan effects, I included *Presidential Election* years and *Party of the President*. I also controlled for *Government Revenue* as a share of GDP, as well as *Unemployment*. These two measures should capture the impact of automatic stabilizers on the budget as the economy moves through the business cycle. Finally, because the descriptive data in Figure 3.1 clearly indicate that the budget evolved quite differently following the Korean War buildup than it did in the three other episodes, I included a dummy variable for year and an interactive term (*1950s * Change in Military Spending*) to allow the impact of changes in military spending on the budget to vary before and after 1958. I also estimated the model on a sample that begins in 1959.

The results indicate that military buildups have had a negative impact on the budget balance since 1958 but not during the 1950s (Table 3.1). The main effect of military buildups on the budget balance is signifi-cant and negative for most of the postwar period. However, the signifi-cant interaction term indicates that during the 1950s, changes in military spending had no significant impact on the budget, controlling for other factors. This statistical relationship thus echoes the pattern evident in the descriptive time series we examined earlier: the Korean War buildup was followed by a budget surplus, while buildups in the three other episodes generated large and persistent deficits.

TABLE 3.1. *Military Spending and Budget Deficits*

	1949–2008	1959–2008
Military Spending	−0.04**	−0.04**
	(0.02)	(0.01)
Unemployment	−0.31**	−0.29***
	(0.15)	(0.10)
Revenue	89.64***	125.20***
	(17.47)	(12.66)
Party of the President	−0.25	−0.06
	(0.32)	(0.20)
Election	−0.32	−0.03
	(0.34)	(0.24)
1950 × Military Spending	0.05***	
	(0.02)	
1950	−0.35	
	(0.41)	
Observations	56	48
F Statistic	6.36	26.94
R^2	0.41	0.73

Dependent variable is the Budget Deficit/GDP.
*Significant at 0.1; **significant at 0.05; ***significant at 0.01.

The magnitude of the impact that military buildups have had on the budget since 1959 is substantively important. The typical post-1958 buildup has seen military expenditures increase by between 13 and 25 percent from year t to $t + 1$. The statistical model thus suggests that these one-year increases widen the budget deficit by between 0.5 and 1 percent of GDP, a fairly substantial shock. Recall also that each military buildup is a multiyear event. Thus, the cumulative impact of each buildup is the impact of a number of consecutive year-to-year increases of military spending. Thus, post-1958 military buildups on average have increased the budget deficit by between 1.5 and 3 percent of GDP. Consequently, the estimated impact of military buildups on the budget balance is consistent with the path illustrated by Figure 3.1.

Unsurprisingly, the model indicates that the business cycle plays an important role in driving the budget balance. The negative and statistically significant coefficient on *Unemployment* indicates that a rising unemployment rate widens the budget deficit. The positive and significant coefficient on *Government Revenues* indicates that the deficit widens as revenues fall and improves as revenues rise. Interestingly, the statistically significant coefficients on both *Government Revenue* and *Change in Military Spending* highlight that the expenditure and revenue sides of the budget have not correlated highly since 1958. Regressing change in revenue against changes in military expenditure confirms this, indicating no systematic relationship, even out to a three-year lag. Rather than responding systematically and quickly to changes in military spending, government revenue responds to the overall budget balance. But even here, the response is relatively slow: a deficit has a positive impact on revenues only after two years. This suggests that military buildups generate budget deficits, and concern about overall deficits eventually induces policymakers to increase revenue.

The statistical model provides little indication that the major changes in tax rates by themselves, partisanship, or presidential elections play a systematic role in determining changes in the budget balance. Perhaps surprisingly, the three tax legislation variables almost never returned a statistically significant coefficient. The one exception, the weakly significant coefficient for the 1981 tax cut in the truncated sample, carries the wrong sign; we expect the tax cuts to reduce revenues, not increase them. These results did not change if I removed *Government Revenue* from the model, nor if I estimated the model with only one or combinations of two of these tax cuts included. Nor are the results sensitive to the coding. I created a second set of variables coded 1 for the first three years the tax act was in effect and 0 in all other years. This measure also failed to return statistically significant coefficients. The only specification that returned a significant and correctly signed coefficient was one that omitted *Change in Military Spending*. In this specification, only the 2001 tax cut had a (weakly) significant and negative impact on the budget balance. Yet even here, the 2001 tax cut was not significant in a specification that included *Change in Military Spending* (while omitting the two other tax acts). Thus, the time series model provides little evidence that major tax cuts have had a systematic impact on the budget balance, once we control for other factors.

Finally, the statistical model offers no evidence that either partisan or electoral effects have a systematic impact on the budget balance. Neither *Party of the President* nor *Presidential Election Year* yields a coefficient that approaches conventional levels of statistical significance. These null results emerged consistently across specifications. This finding is not surprising given the status quo bias imparted to the system by its multi-veto player structure, and the resulting tendency for the overwhelming majority of expenditures to change very little from one year to the next. In such a system, we would not expect small changes in the partisan composition of the legislature to have a dramatic impact on the budget.

In general, therefore, postwar military buildups have produced larger and more persistent budget deficits than other political and economic dynamics. Military buildup induced budget deficits have been larger and more persistent than the deficits that arise when the economy slides into recession. Indeed, whereas the deficits generated by the recessions narrow as the economy recovers, buildup-induced deficits persist long into the recovery phase of the business cycle. Military buildups have created larger and more persistent deficits than the three major postwar tax cuts. In fact, we found no systematic evidence, once we control for other factors, that these tax cuts had a systematic impact on the budget balance. Finally, military buildups have had a more powerful impact on the budget than either partisan politics or presidential elections. Postwar budget deficits have thus emerged from two distinct processes: small deficits arise from recessions and recede as the economy recovers; large deficits arise from military buildups and persist for many years. Postwar military buildups, in short, have created the budget deficits that have pushed the politics of deficit reduction to the fore of American politics.

Explaining the Budgetary Consequences of Military Buildups

Military buildups have generated large and persistent deficits because of the nature of bargaining over budget adjustment within American political institutions. We know surprisingly little about how politics shape the way America finances its military buildups. Perhaps the lack of scholarly attention to this issue reflects a widely shared belief that the answer is pretty simple: politicians borrow rather than tax because taxes are unpopular with voters. As Flores-Macias and Kreps (2013: 836) summarize, "all things being equal, leaders have incentives to finance the cost of war through measures that expose the populace less directly to the cost of conflict, such as borrowing or increasing the money supply." Yet, the "taxes are unpopular" hypothesis is problematic. The United States enacted new taxes immediately to finance its largest postwar buildup – the Korean War – and enacted a large Vietnam surtax in 1968 (and a smaller tax in 1966). Moreover, in the two other buildups, at least one veto player sought to pay for the additional military power with higher taxes. Thus, some American politicians have tried to pay

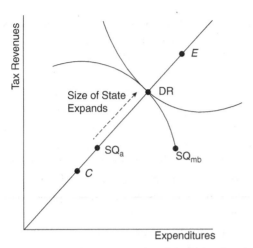

FIGURE 3.4. Persistence of Deficit Reduction Agreements.

consequence, the expected length of a war of attrition rises in line with the value of the prize relative to the cost of fighting.[2] In theory, wars of attrition could last forever, if the prize was very large and the cost of fighting very small.

In negotiations over the budget adjustments, the value of the prize rises because the question of how to reduce a temporary deficit becomes fused to the more fundamental issue of the size and role of the state, in the American economy. As Flores-Macias and Kreps (2013: 837) have noted, "wars become opportunities to shift, sometimes permanently, the allocation of a large volume of resources" (see also Mayhew 2005). The spatial model highlights why adjustment of a temporary budget deficit can permanently (or at least persistently) alter the size of the state (see Figure 3.4). First, every balanced budget outcome that C and L both prefer to SQ_{mb} yields a tax and spending combination, such as DR in Figure 3.4, that is substantially larger than SQ_a. Thus, all of the jointly preferred measures, given the decision to increase military spending, increase the size of the state. Second, this larger state will persist because once selected it becomes an equilibrium outcome given the distribution of preferences and power. As a result, the multiveto player system transforms bargaining to adjust the budget in response to a temporary deficit

---

[2] The probability of fighting in period t is $p = V/(V + C)$, where V is the value of the prize and C is the cost of fighting. The probability of the war of attrition persisting to period $n + 1$ is $p^2 n$.

into bargaining over the size and role of the American state. This raises the value of the outcome substantially above what it would be if the outcome were simply a matter of a temporary increase in taxes or reduction in nonmilitary spending.

In this context, veto players have strong incentives to block the others' proposals. L will block any attempt by C to adjust by cutting social welfare programs because it recognizes that even "temporary" cuts will persist and thus reduce the economic role of the American state. C will block all tax increase proposals by L for the same reason; a temporary tax increase will be difficult to remove once the conflict ends and will thus yield a larger post-conflict state than C is willing to accept without fighting. Altering the size of the state once a deficit-reduction agreement is reached will require more fundamental changes to the distribution of preferences across the political system. L must be replaced by a veto player substantially more conservative for C to reduce state size back to its size prior to the military buildup. Bargaining over adjustment to a temporary military buildup thus becomes fused to deeper conflict over the appropriate size of and role for the state in the American economy.

The fusion of a temporary deficit to deeply seated differences over the appropriate size of the state transforms the nature of bargaining over deficit reduction and transforms the strategies each player is likely to adopt. Conservatives will commit to a no new taxes strategy, preferring to accept the temporary deficit rather than risk a permanent increase in the size of the state. And the conservatives will insist on adjustment via cuts in nonmilitary programs as an attempt to bring the budget deficit back toward balance. Liberals are likely to commit to a no cuts in social program strategy, preferring to accept the temporary deficit rather than risk a permanent cut in welfare-state expenditures. They will insist on bringing the budget back toward balance via higher taxes. Because agreement on how to adjust the budget in response to a temporary deficit has persistent consequences for the size of the state, both players insist on deficit reduction agreements that shift the status quo either vertically or horizontally.

This bargaining framework thus suggests that military buildups have generated large and persistent budget deficits because although administration officials and congressional leaders have agreed on the need for additional military power, they have disagreed about how to pay for it. One branch sought to pay for the additional military expenditures by increasing taxes while the other wanted to cut spending in social welfare programs. The value attached to these short-term measures was magnified by the recognition that any package would have persistent consequences for the size and role of the American state in the economy.

The Politics of Delayed Adjustment

This bargaining framework accurately characterizes how the dynamics of executive branch–congressional conflict transformed the three post–Korean War military buildups into large and persistent budget deficits. In each episode, key congressional leaders and the administration held very different preferences over how to pay for the additional military expenditures. In the wake of the decision to escalate America's involvement in Vietnam, the administration wanted adjustment via tax increases while the key congressional player wanted adjustment via cuts in social welfare programs. The Johnson administration wanted to pay for the additional military expenditures by raising taxes. Johnson's principal economic advisors, including Chairman of the Council of Economic Advisors Gardner Ackley, the Secretary of the Treasury Henry Fowler, and the Budget Director Charles Schultze argued in late 1965 that the additional military expenditures required additional tax revenues (King 1985: 690). The consensus extended into the National Security Council, where Johnson's deputy national security advisor Francis Bator reinforced the call for higher taxes (Bator 1965). Neither Johnson nor his close advisors wanted to cut nonmilitary expenditures. They recognized that any expenditure cuts would come from Johnson's Great Society programs, and Johnson was quite unwilling to allow the war in Vietnam to undermine his domestic war on poverty.

Though many congressional leaders shared Johnson's commitment to the Great Society and supported additional taxes to pay for the war-related costs, some veto players did not. Wilbur Mills, Chairman of the House Ways and Means Committee, was especially important. Mills strongly preferred adjustment via cuts in nonmilitary expenditures. Mills' preference for expenditure cuts rested in part on short-term considerations about the inflationary impact of the buildup. Rather than raise taxes, therefore, Mills wanted to adjust by cutting current and future spending in nonmilitary programs.

Key veto players had equally distant ideal points in the wake of the buildup sparked by the Soviet invasion of Afghanistan. The Reagan administration, which assumed office in January 1981, preferred to reduce the budget deficit by cutting nonmilitary expenditures and keeping tax rates unchanged. The administration's orientation was well summarized by Reagan himself following a series of meetings with the congressional leadership in early March of 1982. "I believe it's time for you and me together to tell the Congress: 'No, you may not touch our tax cut'" (Weisman 1982). The House leadership held opposing preferences. The Democratic majority leadership, and especially Speaker of the House Tip O'Neil, the Chairman of the House Ways and Means Committee Dan Rostenkowski, and Chairman of the House Appropriations Committee Jamie Whitten, preferred adjustment through cuts in military spending and higher taxes and strongly opposed cuts in nonmilitary programs. O'Neill was a committed New Deal Democrat with strong allegiance to the Great Society programs that Johnson had created. "I've been one of the big spenders of all time," he told a gathering of reporters in early 1981 (Farrell 2001: 563). As O'Neill wrote in his memoirs, "I've always believed in our responsibility as a nation to pay for the health and welfare of the American people. Yes, I've supported higher taxes, but it's those taxes that made possible the tremendous progress we've seen" (O'Neill 1987: 378). Rostenkowski was a bit to the right of Speaker O'Neill; he believed the constraints on the growth of spending had to be a central element of budgetary adjustments. But he also remained supportive of expanded healthcare expenditures and the other elements of the welfare state.

A similar gap characterized the bargaining environment following the attacks of September 11. The Bush administration wanted to move back toward a balanced budget via cuts in nonmilitary discretionary expenditures and by slowing the growth of entitlement expenditures (Medicaid and Medicare in particular, though Medicare Part D is an obvious exception) (Office of Management and Budget 2004; Schatz 2004). In Congress, the key veto players consisted of a small group of moderate Republican senators, including the senators from Maine, Susan Collins and Olympia Snowe; Lincoln Chaffee (RI); and George J. Voinovich (OH). According to the American Conservative Union, Snowe and Collins voted the conservative position one-third of the time and Chaffee only 12 percent of the time in 2005. In 2006, Chaffee voted the conservative position 24 percent of the time; Snowe, 36 percent; and Collins, 48 percent. Americans for Democratic Action (ADA) report scores of 65 for Collins and Snowe in 2005 and 75 for Chaffee. In 2006, Chaffee's score rose to 80, while Collins and Snowe both recorded 45. Voinovich held moderate positions on the budget in spite of being less moderate overall. Gordon Smith (R-OR) supported them on some occasions. All four senators supported existing entitlement programs and were thus reluctant to balance the budget via sharp expenditure reductions. These moderates preferred to move back toward a balanced budget by increasing taxes.

The congressional leadership and the executive branch thus held very different preferences over how to adjust the budget to accommodate the increased military expenditures they all agreed were necessary. In two cases, the administration pushed for adjustment via cuts in social welfare spending while the congressional leadership preferred adjustment via increased tax revenues. In the third case, the preferences were reversed; congressional veto players pushed for cuts in social welfare programs while the administration pushed for higher taxes. Thus, although all participants recognized the need for adjustment, they disagreed fairly sharply about how to adjust.

Because veto players held such different preferences, executive–congressional bargaining over the choice of an adjustment package was characterized by distributive conflict that delayed adjustment for years. The recognition that congressional leaders wanted expenditure cuts contributed to Johnson's decision that his best strategy was patience – wait until the budget deficit was so large that congressional leadership cared more about reducing the deficit than they did about how they did so. Moreover, Johnson believed that asking for a tax increase too soon would cause the congressional leadership to dig in. As he told Robert McNamara in May 1966: "if I indicated I had to have taxes ... this would drive [Wilbur] Mills and [Russell] Long to a position that is irrevocable that will make them ... in concrete against a tax bill" (Executive Office of the President of the United States 1966; King 1985). In an effort to avoid being pressured for expenditure cuts, therefore, Johnson delayed calling for a tax increase until the 10 percent surtax he included in the 1967 State of the Union address, and then delayed submitting legislation to Congress that requested a tax increase until August of 1967 (Johnson 1967).

Once Johnson did request a tax increase, Wilbur Mills engineered a 20 to 5 vote against it in the House Ways and Means Committee. In doing so, Mills communicated to the administration that he would allow Congress to consider the administration's proposed tax increase once Johnson found more than $6 billion in cuts in current nonmilitary spending and additional cuts in planned spending. Determined to protect its Great Society programs, the administration refused to accept the expenditure cuts that Mills sought. Johnson's budget director, Charles L. Schultze,

told Johnson that Mills was playing chicken; if Johnson took an unyielding position, Mills would back down (Collins 1996: 404). Thus, Johnson
adopted an unyielding position. By late 1967, therefore, more than two
years after the decision to escalate U.S. involvement in Vietnam had been
taken, the effort to adjust the budget was deadlocked. Johnson and Mills
held fast to their preferred adjustment paths in the belief that the other
guy would blink first.

Strategic bargaining between the congressional leadership and administration officials delayed the adoption of deficit reduction measures
during 1980s as well (McCubbins 1991). The two sides made an initial attempt to reduce the budget deficit in the early spring of 1982
(Fuerbringer 1982; Tolchin 1982b). Veto players agreed on a few key
issues. The administration accepted the need for additional revenue, but
was unwilling to accept the repeal of the third stage of its major tax
cut, scheduled to take effect in July 1983. House Democrats recognized
the need for some expenditure cuts, but were unwilling to cut scheduled increases in Social Security payments. Yet, the two sides remained
far apart. The congressional Democrats proposed $145 billion additional
revenue over the next three fiscal years, but the administration would
accept only $110 billion. The administration proposed $25 billion in
cuts, while congressional Democrats were willing to accept only half this
amount. Positions were reversed on military spending, with congressional Democrats seeking $33 billion in reductions and the administration
willing to accept only $23 billion. (see Tolchin 1982a). By May, negotia-
tions had deadlocked.

Failure to reach agreement in the spring of 1982 precipitated a
five-year struggle. Each year presented the same fundamental story. The
administration would propose a budget that contained a large deficit;
Congress would reject the administration's budget and write its own version. The administration would threaten to veto any budget that sharply
raised taxes or substantially reduced military expenditures. For five years,
"[b]oth parties called the deficits a scandal but could not agree on how
to reduce them. The president remained adamantly against any further
tax increases and held tenaciously to his defense buildup. The [House]
Democrats wanted Social Security shielded from budget cutters and dug in
their heels opposing further domestic program cuts" (LeLoup 2005: 82).
Some progress came in late 1985 in connection with Gramm–Rudman–
Hollings (Havens 1986; West 1988). But, Gramm–Rudman "proved to
be no panacea to the executive-legislative deadlock of the previous four
years. Virtually every deadline in the new timetable was missed ... While

GR communicated to the public that budget deficits were the number one legislative priority, it did not foster long-term solutions to deficit reduction" (LeLoup and Hancock 1988: 44–45). Thus, six full years after the military buildup began, the executive branch and Congress remained unable to agree on how to balance the budget.

Identical bargaining dynamics transformed the War on Terror buildup into a persistent budget deficit during the 2000s. Indeed, in this episode, disagreement between the executive branch and the congressional leadership was so intense that it resulted in "the great unraveling" of the budget process (Rubin 2007). Disagreement over the path of adjustment made it impossible to shift the budget far from the status quo in any direction. Any attempt by Senate moderates to raise taxes, directly or indirectly, met opposition from administration officials and the conservative Republicans that dominated the House. Each year posed slightly different issues, but each instance effectively reduced to the same underlying conflict. The Bush administration and House Republicans wanted large tax cuts and significant reductions in nonmilitary expenditures. Senate moderates, along with Senate Democrats, wanted to maintain social programs and minimize further tax cuts. Kent Conrad succinctly summarized the problem, "Democrats don't want to cut or reduce Medicare or the other entitlements. Republicans don't want to abandon any tax cut" (Dennis 2007: 466).

In March of 2004, for example, the moderate Senate Republicans (Snowe, Collins, Chafee, and John McCain) voted with the Democrats to reinstate pay as you go rules (the so-called Feingold Amendment). This amendment would ensure that any tax cut be offset by matching cuts in expenditures. The House leadership and the Bush administration refused to accept PAYGO because the measure would complicate efforts to make permanent the 2001 tax cuts (Taylor 2004). Similarly, all attempts to cut entitlement expenditures encountered strenuous Senate objection. For example, in its 2005 budget, the administration proposed cutting Medicaid spending by $14 billion over five years. The House Budget Committee added further cuts, reaching a total of about $69 billion over five years. The Senate Budget Committee pared the House cuts to only $32 billion. And even this figure was too large for the Senate's moderate Republicans. Gordon Smith (R-OR) proposed an amendment that stripped out language instructing the Finance Committee to find $15 billion of reductions in the growth of mandatory programs over five years. Senate Democrats and six additional Republicans supported Smith's amendment (Schuler 2005). In the end, and in the face of a forecast budget deficit of more than $400 billion per year, the House and Senate agreed to cut $32 billion over five years (Taylor 2005). Thus, five years after the terrorist attacks of 9/11 and the resulting increase of military spending in support of wars in Afghanistan and Iraq, the administration and Congress remained unable to agree on how to move the budget back toward balance.

Finally, in each of the three buildups, disagreement between the administration and Congress over how to address a temporary budget deficit became fused with more profound differences over the appropriate role of the state in the American economy. Throughout 1965–1967, Johnson's commitment to higher taxes was reinforced by his determination to construct an expanded welfare state as his legacy. Having succeeded in enacting the Economic Opportunity Act in 1964 and the Social Security Amendments establishing Medicare and Medicaid in 1965, Johnson became unwilling to accept even "temporary" cuts in program spending to pay for the Vietnam War because he recognized that any such cuts could not be undone easily once war-related expenditures ended. Wilbur Mills likewise linked the issue of how to pay for temporary expenditures to deeper concerns about the size of the state. Mills believed that higher taxes enacted to pay for Vietnam would persist: "Congress would use the additional tax revenue as an excuse to finance new domestic programs once the conflict in Vietnam subsided" (Zelizer 2000: 263). This eventually in turn "would mean bigger and bigger government with a smaller and smaller range of freedom of activity for the private sector" (Collins 1996: 403). Thus, conflict between Johnson and Mills over how to pay for the Vietnam War was not simply a battle over how to pay for temporary emergency expenditures, but triggered more profound differences over the appropriate size of the American state. Both men dug in their heels because both believed that the decision about how to pay for the Vietnam War would have persistent consequences for the economic role of the state in the American economy.

Different ideas about the appropriate role of the state in the American economy became fused with deficit reduction negotiations during the 1980s and 2000s as well. By the 1980s, however, using deficit reduction negotiations to reduce the size of the American welfare state had become a central element of Republican strategy (Krugman 2007a). Conservatives opposed to the expanded welfare state converged around a "starve the beast" strategy during the late 1970s (Bartlett 2007). The logic of the strategy was to create a budget deficit, hold fast to a "no tax increase" bargaining position, and force cuts in social welfare spending. Senator Daniel Moynihan, in a *New York Times* opinion piece, accused the Reagan administration of embracing this strategy to roll back the social welfare programs (Moynihan 1985). Although evidence that the Reagan administration enacted the 1981 tax cut intentionally to create a budget deficit is inconclusive (Prasad 2012), the administration certainly viewed deficit reduction negotiations as an opportunity to trim social welfare programs as part of its broader strategy to roll back the welfare state. Recognizing this element of administration strategy, congressional Democrats fought hard to defend the increased welfare state they had achieved since the early 1930s.

The Bush administration seems to have embraced the strategy of starve the beast even more firmly. Only weeks after the inauguration, an administration presentation called "Blueprint for New Beginnings" highlighted its approach to the budget. One prominent chart carried the title: "Budget Surpluses Lead to Bigger Government," thereby making clear that preventing an expansion of the state was a central consideration behind the administration's 2001 tax cut (Schick 2003: 6). Though we cannot know whether the administration would have engineered a large deficit as part of this starve the beast strategy in the absence of the War on Terror, it is fairly clear that once the budget deficit emerged in 2003 and 2004 the administration embraced the need for adjustment as an opportunity to achieve cuts in social welfare programs. Opposition to this strategy, at least through 2007, was centered in the Senate, where moderate Republicans joined with Senate Democrats to resist the administration's efforts to roll back central elements of the welfare state.

The dynamics of strategic bargaining between the executive branch and Congress has thus transformed military buildups that all agreed were necessary into large and persistent budget deficits that nobody desired. In the three post–Korean War military buildups, differences between the administration and congressional leaders over how to adjust – by raising taxes or by reducing social welfare spending – has greatly complicated the effort to enact quickly deficit reduction measures. Moreover, the differences that complicated bargaining over the solution to a temporary budget deficit were reinforced by sharply opposing perspectives concerning the appropriate role for the state in the American economy. This fusion was in some instances opportunistic, in some instances programmatic, but in all instances shaped by the recognition that decisions made to correct a temporary deficit would be transformed by the status quo bias of the American political system into persistent outcomes. As a result, deficit reduction occurred years after the increased military expenditures rendered it necessary.

The Korean War and Rapid Budget Adjustment

The political response to the Korean War military buildup fails to fit this pattern. Although military spending increased sharply, the increases did not generate a large and persistent budget deficit. Although it is tempting to view this case as one that challenges the bargaining framework and thus offers useful advice concerning how to avoid such bargaining deadlocks, in fact, this episode fits firmly within the standard framework. It does so because the political environment within which policymakers responded to the Korean War buildup differed in two important ways from the subsequent episodes.

The first and most fundamental difference was that the ideal points of the Truman administration and the congressional leadership were so similar that any differences in preferred adjustment packages were unimportant: all preferred to pay for the Korean War by increasing taxes sharply. Truman was fiscally conservative. This conservative orientation reflected Truman's wartime experience as Chair of the Senate Special Committee to Investigate the National Defense Program, a position at the center of the World War II mobilization effort. Truman came to believe that Roosevelt had borrowed too heavily to finance war-related expenditures and, as a consequence, had added more than was necessary to the national debt (Donovan 1996: 325). Truman spelled out the administration's preference in a July 19, 1950, message to Congress: "the increased appropriations ... will mean sharply increased Federal expenditures. For this reason, we should increase Federal Revenues more sharply than I have previously recommended ... We must make every effort to finance the greatest possible amount of needed expenditures by taxation. The increase of taxes is our basic weapon in offsetting the inflationary pressures exerted by enlarged government expenditures" (Truman 1950).

Key congressional leaders also preferred higher taxes. The Congressional Joint Committee on the Economic Report, for instance, quickly pronounced itself in favor of a sharp tax increase. Increased military expenditures must be paid for by enacting "a tax bill that will finance the expense without increasing the debt" (Pierpaoli 1999: 33–34). Even those who were otherwise the staunchest critics of the Truman administration, Robert Taft and the nationalist Republicans, agreed on the need to pay for the Korean conflict by raising taxes as quickly as possible. Taft asserted that Soviet aggression was pushing the United States "into a normal condition in which about 20 percent of [its] national production will be devoted to" the military. Because this new state of affairs was persistent, the government should "tax the people" to pay for the entire amount (Whitney 1950: 1). Key committee chairmen, including Robert L. Doughton, the Chair of House Ways and Means Committee, and the Senate Finance Committee chair, Walter F. George, also supported higher taxes. Doughton told a business leader in his district that he had met with Senator George and Secretary of Treasury Snyder yesterday and agreed "to take the Tax Bill which the House has passed and which is now before the Senate Finance Committee and amend that bill rather than to start a new bill ... Secretary Snyder suggested that the increased tax on corporations and individuals might be made retroactive for a part of 1950 – perhaps the last quarter or something like that" (Doughton 1950a). Doughton communicated his support for higher taxes to finance the military buildup in a series of letters written to the business elite in his district in July 1950 (Doughton 1950b). Thus, the ideal points of the relevant veto players clustered quite closely together around a balance budget achieved via higher taxes.

Because the administration and the congressional leadership agreed on how to pay for the additional military expenditures, they enacted the necessary legislation very quickly. A first tax bill was introduced in the fall of 1950. The House had passed legislation in the spring of 1950 that reduced World War II–related excise taxes. This bill was sitting in the Senate Finance Committee at the time of North Korea's invasion. By August of 1950, the Senate had transformed the House bill into a tax increase that it sent back to the House. Once in the House, the legislation moved quickly through the conference committee and was enacted into law. Truman and Congress enacted a second tax increase, this one on excess profits, later in 1950 (Romer and Romer 2008: 23). A third tax increase followed in 1951 as part of the normal budget process. Thus, with few differences separating the administration and the congressional leadership, legislation that raised taxes was enacted in tandem with rising military expenditures.

Second, the absence of substantively important differences over how to adjust the budget between the administration and congressional leaders might have been assisted by the relatively limited role the state played in the American economy. On the one hand, total government expenditures in 1949 – thus not including the exception spending in response to the North Korean invasion – were only 14 percent of GDP. Thus, in 1949 the American state was only two-thirds the size it would attain by the late 1970s, that is, once Johnson's Great Society programs were in place and Vietnam War–related expenditures had ended. On the other hand, welfare-related programs comprised a very small share of the total. Social Security and Income Security programs combined for about 15 percent, and health-related expenditures (excluding veterans' benefits) accounted for only 1 percent. In contrast, defense spending, international programs, and veterans' benefits consumed 62 percent of government spending. Interest payments on debt, most of which had been accumulated during World War II, claimed an additional 13 percent of government expenditures. Thus, not only did the state play a very small role in the American economy, but social welfare programs in addition constituted a very small share of spending. As a consequence, not only were there no welfare programs that could be cut to pay for the Korean War, but there was also little incentive to link bargaining over war finance to differences concerning the appropriate role of the state in the American economy.

Rather than contradict the bargaining framework, therefore, the Korean War buildup provides additional evidence to support this framework. The Korean War buildup failed to generate a large and persistent budget deficit because the Truman administration and the congressional leadership agreed to pay for this war with a sharp increase in tax revenues. Rapid agreement between the administration and Congress to raise taxes emerged within an environment in which the Truman and the congressional leadership both preferred higher taxes to cuts to nonmilitary programs. Such support for higher taxes and the lack of consideration given to other strategies may have been facilitated by the absence of a welfare state that could be scaled back to free up revenue and further reinforced by concern that the debt accumulated during World War II was already too heavy a burden for the American economy.

Conclusion

Postwar military buildups have pushed deficit reduction to the fore of American politics. They have done so by generating the largest and most persistent budget deficits that the United States has experienced in this period. Although the federal government has recorded budget deficits for most of the postwar period, variation in the magnitude of these deficits has resulted from two processes. The business cycle has tended to generate relatively small and short-lived deteriorations of the budget. The budget deficit widens by a bit less than 1 percent of GDP as the economy moves into recession and then narrows rapidly as the economy moves into the expansionary phase. In contrast, military buildups have generated relatively large and long-lived deficits. Buildups have widened the deficit by between 1.5 and 3 percent of GDP, and these buildup-induced deficits have persisted for four or more years. Because they have generated large budget deficits, military buildups undertaken in response to exogenous security shocks have pushed the politics of deficit reduction to the fore.

Bargaining between administrations and congressional leaders to reduce budget deficits generated by military buildups has been conflictual. Conflict has characterized bargaining over adjustment because key policymakers held differing preferences over the possible adjustment packages. In the 1960s, Johnson wanted to adjust via temporary increases in tax revenue; Mills wanted to cut spending. In the 1980s and 2000s, Republican administrations wanted to reduce the budget deficit by cuts in social welfare spending, while congressional leaders, Democrats almost exclusively during the 1980s and Democrats and moderate Republicans during the 2000s, sought increases in tax revenues. Different preferences over how to adjust led to intense conflictual bargaining that delayed the enactment of an adjustment package by several years. Budget adjustment in the Korean War conflict failed to fit the pattern, but not the model. In this case, the administration and the congressional leadership agreed that the costs of the Korean War should be borne by current income and quickly implemented the necessary legislation.

Bargaining conflict has been aggravated by the recognition by administration officials and congressional leaders that adjustment of the budget to a temporary spending shock can have persistent consequences for the size of the state in the American economy. Wilbur Mills' based his opposition to Johnson's desired tax increase in part on the concern that higher taxes to pay for the war would lead to a larger state after the war as revenues were diverted to other uses. Johnson's reluctance to consider cuts in Great Society programs was based on his belief that such cuts would be permanent rather than last only as long as the war. The Reagan and Bush administrations appeared to use the buildup-induced deficit as leverage with which to reduce the size of the state by cutting nonmilitary programs. Opposition to this strategy by Democrats and moderate Republicans was inspired in part by the recognition that these cuts too would be permanent and thus contributed to the delay in adjustment. Hence, bargaining to reduce temporary deficits generated by increased military spending that all agreed was necessary became fused to more profound differences over the appropriate size and role of the state in the American economy. The recognition that measures enacted to reduce a temporary deficit would have persistent consequences made all parties reluctant to make concessions, and thereby extended the time required to rein in the deficit.

4

Military Buildups, Financial Power, and America's Postwar Booms

> The events that lead to a crisis start with ... some ... outside shock to the macroeconomic system.
>
> Charles P. Kindleberger[1]

America's deficit-financed military buildups have had a powerful impact on its postwar macroeconomic performance. Three of the American economy's four longest postwar economic expansions have occurred in the midst of, and were triggered by, the three post–Korean War military buildups, all of which, as we have seen, were paid for by running large budget deficits. These postwar booms have been responsible for a considerable share of the increased prosperity the American economy has generated since World War II. In each instance, the unemployment rate has been cut in half over the course of the boom. And each boom has raised per capita income by about 22 percent, on average, although since the 1980s these income gains have been unevenly distributed. Deficit-financed military buildups have thus ushered in extended periods of exceptional prosperity. These booms have also carried less welcome consequences. They have been associated with an overvalued dollar, which in trade-adjusted terms has appreciated by about 30 percent during each boom. Buildups have been accompanied by deteriorating current account balances.

America's deficit-financed military buildups have generated economic booms because of America's global financial power. American financial power is generally seen to derive from the dollar's position at the center

---

[1] Kindleberger and Aliber (2005: 25).

of the international monetary system as a reserve and vehicle currency. As Cohen (2006: 45) notes, the dollar's international centrality creates a sustained global demand for dollar denominated assets. The United States' position at the center of the international financial system enables American residents to attract foreign capital in large volumes at low interest rates for extended periods. As a result, when the American demand for capital rises, the United States simply attracts a larger share of total cross-border capital flows. Because the United States can import large volumes of capital from the rest of the world for extended periods, the persistent budget deficits that result from military buildups do not crowd out private investment. Instead, buildup-induced fiscal shocks appear to stimulate investment. The combination of a persistent fiscal stimulus and robust private investment transforms what might otherwise be a typical expansion into an extended economic boom.

This chapter builds this argument in two steps. It first demonstrates that postwar military buildups have generated economic booms. I draw on open economy macroeconomics to develop expectations concerning the impact of budget deficits on output, the real exchange rate, and the current account. I then evaluate these expectations using descriptive and inferential statistics. Next, I focus on the sources and consequences of America's financial power. I explain how American financial power derives from the interaction between attributes of American financial markets and the network characteristics of global finance. I then develop a time-varying measure that captures the degree to which the United States has exploited its financial power and demonstrate that the United States has leveraged this power each time it has embarked on a military buildup. Finally, I demonstrate that because of its financial power, America's deficit-financed military buildups have not crowded out private investment but have instead sparked investment booms.

The Macroeconomic Consequences of Military Buildups: Theoretical Considerations

The prevailing tendency in the American policymaking community, as well as among the Washington, DC think tanks that focus on the international economy, is to attribute American external imbalances to the policies and practices of foreign governments. Ben Bernanke (2005) argued that American imbalances during the 2000s were a product of the interaction between high savings rates and the search for low-risk assets in

East Asian economies. Other commentators attributed East Asia's high savings rates to underdeveloped national financial markets (Clarida 2005). During the 1980s, American policymakers and commentators argued that American current account deficits were due to similar structural weaknesses in Japan. Hence, and perhaps ironically, American policymakers argued that not even its trade deficits were made in America.

Other analysts argue that America's external deficits have domestic roots. This "twin deficit" explanations draw on standard open economic macroeconomic models that highlight the extent to which government budget deficits cause national savings to fall, and thereby cause the current account to deteriorate (Bluedorn and Leigh 2011; Chinn 2005; Chinn and Hiro 2008; Corsetti and Mueller 2006). The demand shock that budget deficits impart might further weaken the current account by encouraging investment to increase in response to the buoyant demand. I argue that the "twin deficits" have been a defining characteristic of American postwar political economy; the deficits generated by buildups as well as the booms they spark have been the primary cause of American external deficits. We look first at some theoretical considerations and then turn to the empirical record.

Theoretical Considerations

We can understand how fiscal policy affects macroeconomic activity with a standard Mundell–Fleming model of an open economy with capital mobility. This workhorse macroeconomic model suggests that given at least partial capital mobility, the impact of fiscal policy on aggregate demand varies across exchange rate regimes. Fiscal policy has a large impact on output under a fixed exchange rate. Under a floating exchange rate regime, however, the impact of fiscal policy depends on the size of the economy. In a small open economy, fiscal policy has no impact on aggregate demand but does affect the exchange rate. In a large open economy, however, fiscal policy affects aggregate demand and the exchange rate. We look at each case.

We look first at the impact of fiscal policy in an open economy with a fixed exchange rate. These expectations should characterize the Vietnam War buildup. In this case fiscal policy has a powerful impact on domestic demand. The initial fiscal expansion increases aggregate demand and pushes up the domestic interest rate as the additional government borrowing increases the demand for loanable funds. This additional demand has two consequences for the balance of payments. First, the current account deteriorates as imports rise and exports fall in response to the higher demand. Second, higher interest rates attract capital inflows in excess of the deterioration of the current account, thereby giving rise to an overall balance of payments surplus. The balance of payments surplus in turn places upward pressure on the domestic currency. Because the government is committed to maintaining the peg, the monetary authority must intervene in the foreign exchange market, thereby expanding the supply of the local currency. By defending the peg in this way, therefore, an expansionary fiscal expansion forces a monetary expansion as well. The combination of fiscal and monetary expansion imparts a powerful demand stimulus to the macroeconomy. Over time, the expansion of the money supply in the face of persistent balance of payments surpluses will generate inflation that in turn causes a real exchange rate appreciation.

With a floating exchange rate, the impact of a fiscal expansion depends on the size of the economy. In the case of a small open economy, fiscal expansion has no impact on economic output. In this case, fiscal expansion has a positive impact on aggregate demand and pushes up the domestic interest rate as the government deficit increases the demand for loanable funds. Higher domestic interest rates attract foreign capital, and capital inflows cause the currency to appreciate. As the currency strengthens, domestic residents purchase more imports, and domestic producers sell less abroad. This decline of net exports reduces aggregate demand, thus offsetting the increased demand imparted by the fiscal expansion. In a small open economy, therefore, a fiscal expansion produces an appreciated currency and a larger current account deficit, but has no impact on output.

In a large open economy with a floating exchange rate, however, fiscal policy affects output. The key factor that distinguishes a large from a small open economy is the extent to which local developments affect the world interest rate. A small open economy takes the world interest rate as given. Thus, a larger budget deficit in a small open economy increases domestic interest rates but not the world interest rate. In contrast, policy changes in a large open economy affect the world interest rate. The decision to run a larger budget deficit, by imparting a significant change to global demand for global savings, has an impact on world interest rates. As a result, fiscal expansion affects output. The distinction is of more than theoretical importance, for a considerable body of empirical work indicates that the United States is a large economy: its fiscal policy decisions affect world interest rates (Bayoumi and Swiston 2010; Ehrmann and Fratzscher 2005; Ehrmann, Fratzscher, and Rigobon 2007, 2011).

We can walk through the steps by which fiscal policy affects output in a large open economy. The initial fiscal expansion increases the world interest rate, but by less than it increases the local interest rate. The emergence of the gap between domestic and world interest rates attracts foreign capital. The foreign capital inflows cause the local currency to appreciate. And this appreciation ends when the local and world interest rates once again equal each other. However, because the initial gap between rates is smaller in the case of the large economy, the currency appreciates by less than in the case of the small economy. As a result, the reduction of demand caused by currency appreciation is less than the increased demand imparted by the fiscal expansion. Fiscal expansion thus increases output.

The Mundell–Fleming model thus suggests that the budget deficits generated by military buildups are likely to have had an impact on America's postwar macroeconomic performance. These fiscal expansions are likely to have increased output, caused the real exchange rate to appreciate, reduced net exports, and increased net capital inflows (Yellen 1989). And though the theoretical presentation relies on a simple comparative statics framework, we can embed this in a broader temporal frame. As we saw in Chapter 3, military buildups have generated large and sustained budget deficits; these deficits persist for three to seven years. Hence, postwar military buildups have generated persistent fiscal expansions. Thus, we expect them to generate persistent increases in aggregate demand, persistent current account weakness as well as the capital inflows required to finance these external deficits, and persistent currency appreciation. We turn now to evaluate these expectations.

Descriptive Statistics

The impact that deficit-financed military buildups have had on America's postwar macroeconomic performance is clearly visible in descriptive statistics (see Figure 4.1). Deficit-financed military buildups spark an economic boom by imparting persistent pro-cyclical stimulus to economic activity. This stimulus, which we saw was about 2 percent of gross domestic product (GDP), acts in conjunction with the increased economic activity it sparks to strengthen the dollar substantially in real terms. The combination of a domestic boom and an overvalued currency in turn weaken the external balance. The booms, currency misalignments, and external imbalances dissipate as policymakers narrow the budget deficit. Only the Korean War buildup failed to generate an economic boom and its associated imbalances.

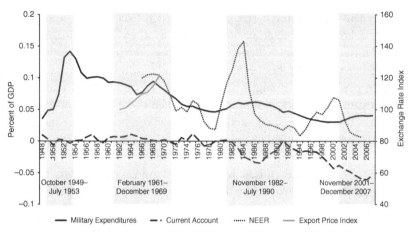

FIGURE 4.1. Buildups, Booms, and Imbalances.

We can look more closely at some of the bivariate relationships to appreciate the strength of these relationships across the postwar period. As a first step, notice that military buildups have been highly correlated with economic booms. The American economy experienced eleven economic expansions between 1948 and 2008 (see Table 4.1). Each expansion lasted, on average, just under five years (fifty-eight months); the median length was forty-five months. Looking at the average for all expansions obscures important differences, however. Four postwar expansions have been extraordinarily long: the three booms highlighted in Figure 4.1 and a fourth that began in March of 1991 and ended in March of 2001. The average length of these four postwar booms is ninety-six months. And even if we exclude the 1990s boom, because it is the longest, the average length of the remaining three is still seventy-eight months. In contrast, each of the seven "normal" expansions persisted for thirty-six months. Moreover, the shortest of the four booms, that which ended in December 2007, was more than a full year longer than the longest of the normal expansions.

These booms are highly correlated with postwar military buildups (see Table 4.2). Overall, the presence and absence of a military buildup correctly classifies nine of eleven postwar expansions into the boom and normal expansion categories. The two misclassified cases include one in which a buildup did not spark a boom and one in which a boom was not accompanied by a buildup. The Korean War buildup was not associated with a boom. Yet, as we learned in Chapter 3, the additional military

TABLE 4.1. *U.S. Postwar Economic Expansions*

Trough	Peak	Length in Months
October 1945	November 1948	37
October 1949	July 1953	45
May 1954	August 1957	39
April 1958	April 1960	24
February 1961	December 1969	106
November 1970	November 1973	36
March 1975	January 1980	58
July 1980	July 1981	12
November 1982	July 1990	91
March 1991	March 2001	120
November 2001	December 2007	73
Booms		97.5
Overall average		58.3
All others		35.9

Source: NBER 2009. "Business Cycles and Contractions," http://www.nber.org/cycles.html

TABLE 4.2. *Military Buildups and Expansions*

		Military Buildup	
		Yes	No
Economic Expansions	Boom	3	1
	Normal	1	6

expenditures generated by the Korean War were paid for with a contemporaneous tax increase whereas the three other buildups were debt financed. This suggests that how the government chooses to pay for a military buildup, rather than the buildup itself, is an important factor in determining whether a buildup generates a boom. The tech boom is the second misclassification; this boom was not associated with a military buildup. This suggests that a deficit-financed military buildup may have been a sufficient condition for a postwar economic boom, but not a necessary one. Although the correlation is not perfect, the presence or absence of a military buildup correctly classifies 91 percent of postwar economic expansions as booms and normal expansions.[2]

---

[2] Fisher's exact test indicates that the correlation is significant at 0.02, reasonable given the very small sample.

Military buildups also correlate with changes in relative prices. The real exchange rate clearly illustrates the relative price consequences of postwar booms. In each episode, the budget deficits generated by military buildups and the private sector activity these deficits stimulate caused the dollar to appreciate fairly sharply in real terms. The appreciation is most clearly evident in the 1980s, where the dollar appreciated sharply in real terms as the budget deficit widened. The appreciation, at its peak, is about 50 percent. Similar patterns are evident in the 1960s and 2000s as well. In the 1960s, where the dollar's nominal exchange rate was pegged to gold, we see a real appreciation as inflation created by the booming economy raised U.S. prices relative to America's trade partners. In the 2000s, the Bush buildup slowed the rate at which the dollar depreciated in the wake of the collapsing tech bubble and thus maintained the dollar at an overvalued real rate through the first half of the decade. Moreover, the 2000s may be characterized by regime change such that the effective exchange rate index understates the dollar's real value (Chinn 2005; Chinn and Hiro 2008). The United States financed its large external imbalance throughout this period by borrowing from public and quasi-public entities – sovereign wealth funds in particular. Some of these sovereigns, East Asian governments especially, pegged their currencies to the dollar. As a result, many economists estimated that the dollar was overvalued relative to East Asian currencies by 25 to 40 percent. Indeed, the extent of the dollar over-valuation can be appreciated by the amount of concern about the likelihood of a hard landing. Nouriel Roubini and Brad Setser, for instance, raised the specter in 2005 (Roubini and Setser 2005b), as did Raghuram Rajan (2005), then Director of Research at the International Monetary Fund (IMF) and Obstfeld and Rogoff (2007). Hence, the effective exchange rate index may understate the degree to which the dollar was overvalued after 2003.

Finally, military buildups are highly correlated with persistent large external imbalances. The relationship between military spending shocks and the current account balance is evident in a simple scatterplot. Figure 4.2 plots the ten largest military spending increases and ten largest military spending decreases against the associated changes in the current account balance. The scatterplot exhibits the expected negative relationship: sudden large changes in military spending have been associated with large offsetting changes in the current account balance. Seven of the ten largest military spending increases are associated with large deteriorations of the current account. Five of the ten largest military spending

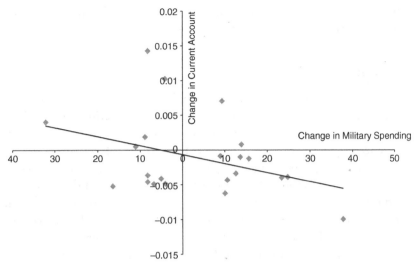

FIGURE 4.2. Military Buildups and the Current Account.

cuts are associated with large improvements in the current account balance. Moreover, with one exception, the observations that don't conform to the expected relationship are the relatively small military spending shocks, and even these observations fall fairly close to the main diagonal. Finally, the relationship evident in the scatterplot comports with prior research. Chinn and Hiro (2008), for instance, find that a 1 percent of GDP change in the budget balance alters the current account by between 0.1 and 0.49 percent of GDP (see also Bartolini and Lahiri 2006; Erceg, Guerrieri, and Gust 2005; Frankel 2006). Thus, most postwar military spending shocks have been offset at least in part by changes in the current account balance.

Military buildups thus appear to be have had a dramatic impact on America's postwar macroeconomic performance. Most military buildups are associated with economic booms, and most postwar booms seem to have been sparked by military buildups. Moreover, over the course of these booms the dollar has strengthened dramatically and the external balance has weakened substantially. It seems, therefore, that buildups have given rise to booms and imbalances. The Korean War buildup stands out as a clear exception to this relationship, but its exceptional nature may be explicable in terms of how the government financed the additional military burdens of hegemony. Because the Truman administration opted to increase taxes rather than borrow, the Korean War buildup didn't impart a substantial aggregate demand shock to the U.S. economy.

Multivariate Analysis

I evaluate the relationship between military buildups and macroeconomic performance in a multivariate setting. Conducting this multivariate analysis is important because existing research finds little robust evidence that U.S. defense spending has had any kind of systematic impact on its postwar macroeconomic performance. As one recent study concludes, "the relationship between defense spending and economic growth in the United States is statistically insignificant regardless of which models are used to examine the relationship" (Heo 2010: 767; see also Kinsella 1990). Because my central claim differs substantially from the conclusion of this established research, I must demonstrate that the relationship I assert exists is evident in a more systematic investigation.

To do so I employ a vector autoregression (VAR) framework. A VAR framework is useful because it allows me to manage the endogeneity present in a complex system such as the macroeconomy (Freeman, Williams, and Lin 1989; Stock and Watson 2001). The typical challenge in a VAR framework is identification: deriving justification for treating one variable as exogenous. Current applications of this approach to the study of U.S. fiscal policy rely on an event-study approach for identification (Blanchard and Perotti 2002; Burnside, Eichenbaum, and Fisher 2004; Edelberg, Eichenbaum, and Fisher 1999; Ramey 2011; Ramey and Shapiro 1998). This approach draws on a set of exogenous fiscal shocks sparked by unexpected large increases in military spending. As Ramey and Shapiro note (1998: 174), "because they are driven by geopolitical shocks, military buildups are likely to be exogenous with respect to [the] macroeconomic variables" of primary interest. Perhaps unsurprisingly, the specific shocks that Ramey and Shapiro employ are those I identified in Chapter 2: Korea 1950, Vietnam 1965, Carter-Reagan 1979/80, and September 11, 2001.

I thus reproduce and extend the Ramey–Shapiro model of the impact of fiscal stimulus on macroeconomic performance. I estimate the following system:

$$Y_t = A(L)Y_{t-1} + U(t)$$

Y_t is a vector of security shocks, defense spending, GDP, fixed investment, real consumption, the current account, and the real effective exchange rate. $A(L)$ is a four-quarter lag operator, and $U(t)$ is a vector of the reduced form errors. In addition, the model incorporates a quadratic time variable. Following Ramey (2011), I order the security shock first. I begin by reproducing Ramey's (2011) findings as a benchmark. I then alter the model specification by using a second coding of the security shock variable and then by the sequential inclusion of the current account balance and the real exchange rate, and then validate that the initial results persist in spite of the altered specification and reduced the sample. I next present impulse response functions from this respecified model to illustrate the impact that security shocks have had on economic growth, the current account, and the real exchange rate.

The core data come from Ramey (Ramey 2012). Data for GDP, investment, consumption, and the current account balance come from the Bureau of Economic Analysis (BEA). Data on GDP and its components cover the full postwar period (1948q1–2008q4). BEA quarterly data on the current account extend back only to 1960q1. I rely on the Federal Reserve Bank's Price Adjusted Broad Dollar Index for my measure of the real exchange rate (Board of Governors of the Federal Reserve System 2013). This index (and every alternative real exchange rate index) has coverage for quarterly intervals only from 1973q1. Thus, the sample period shrinks as I introduce these additional variables into the specification. I code two versions of Security Shock. One version follows Ramey and assigns the value one to 1950q3, 1965q1, 1980q1, and 2001q3 and zero to all other quarters. A second coding assigns the value of 1 to the initial quarter of the shock as well as the subsequent eleven quarters and the value 0 to all other quarters. Hence, this coding assumes that the impact of the military buildup on economic output is not realized exclusively in the first quarter. I follow Ramey (2011) and estimate the system with a four-quarter lag and two time parameters, one that begins in 1948q1 and a second that starts in 1973q2.

We look first at the results generated by the specification that includes the Ramey–Shapiro Security Shock. We see that a security shock has a large and persistent impact on economic growth (Figure 4.3). Across the full postwar era, growth falls briefly following the defense spending shock and then rebounds sharply. Growth peaks four quarters after the shock, and remains positive for four additional quarters – four years in all. The identical trend is evident in the 1960–2008 period once we

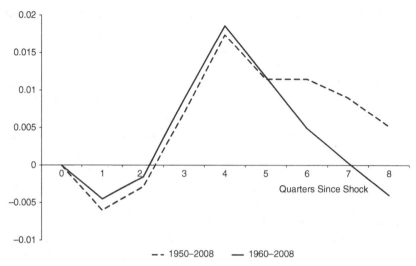

FIGURE 4.3. Security Shocks and Growth.

incorporate the current account balance into the model; shocks trigger
a brief downturn followed by a sharp increase in economic growth that
persists for about two years. Although the estimated response of growth
to the security shock contains considerable uncertainty, the estimate indicates that the security shocks stimulate economic growth for one and a
half to three years.

The models estimated with the extended security shock indicate that
security shocks increase economic output for more than two years. The
peak effect occurs early, roughly two to three quarters after the shock.
In this alternative specification, however, the impact of the buildup persists far longer than the single quarter shock. Whereas the impact in the
Ramey–Shapiro model has dissipated entirely by quarter 8, in this alternative coding the impact of the military buildup on growth persists for
as long as four years. And although the uncertainty associated with this
coding is greater than that surrounding the Ramey–Shapiro coding, the
estimate suggests that even given this heightened uncertainty, the impact
of the military buildup on growth persists for at least ten quarters.

In contrast to much existing research on defense spending and growth,
therefore, my findings indicate that military buildups have had a large,
persistent, and positive impact on economic growth. The discrepancy in
findings is most likely a consequence of different conceptualizations of

the underlying relationship. The established research models the relationship between year-to-year changes in defense spending and annual growth rates. Yet, as we saw in Chapter 2, most year-to-year changes in defense spending are very small – far too small to be expected to have much impact on growth. Moreover, from a basic Keynesian perspective, the driving force should not be military spending per se, but military spending induced budget deficits. My conceptualization corrects for these two considerations by focusing only on the four large postwar buildups. These buildups have been sufficiently large and persistent to affect macroeconomic activity.

The statistical model suggests also that security shocks have had a strong positive impact on the real exchange rate and the current account balance. The real exchange rate begins to appreciate as the defense buildup begins. The currency remains overvalued in real terms twelve quarters after the shock and only then begins to weaken. The currency has returned close to its pre-shock level only after twenty quarters have elapsed. The current account balance deteriorates sharply. As Figure 4.4 illustrates, by the second quarter following the shock, the current account has stabilized at a large deficit, where it remains for about three years. The external balance starts to improve at the end of the third year, the same quarter in which the currency begins to weaken and returns to its pre-shock position after five years. One might be struck by the strong similarity between the estimated persistence of external imbalances and the four-year budget deficits that military buildups produce.

Deficit-financed military buildups have thus had a powerful impact on America's postwar macroeconomic performance. Across the postwar era, military buildups have provided an important source of demand stimulus. The large and persistent budget deficits generated by these buildups have occurred in the midst of ongoing expansionary phases of the business cycle and have transformed what otherwise would have been ordinary economic expansions into booms. Military buildups and the booms they spark have also contributed to large relative price changes via their impact on the dollar. The boom and the real exchange rate appreciation in turn generate large and persistent external imbalances. The Korean War stands out as a clear exception to this pattern, an exception that I suggested was due in large part to the decision to pay for the war via higher taxes now rather than higher taxes in the future.

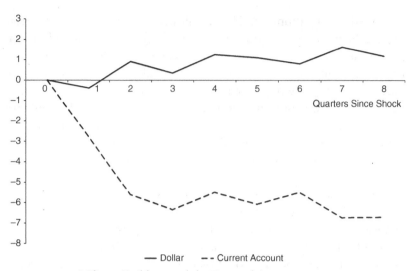

FIGURE 4.4. Military Buildups and the External Account.

Financial Power

Deficit-financed military buildups have generated booms in large part because American financial power allows the U.S. government to borrow heavily for extended periods without crowding out either private investment or consumption. Existing literature conceptualizes financial power in terms of autonomy: the ability to pursue goals for extended periods without encountering financial constraints (Andrews 2006; Cohen 2006). Autonomy arises from the ability to delay current account adjustment for extended periods by attracting capital from the rest of the world for extended periods, at low interest rates (Cohen 2006; Krippner 2011; see also Schwartz 2009; Strange 1989, 1998). As Cohen (2006: 43) explains, "the more liquidity that can be raised externally, either by the government itself or by the private sector, the longer adjustment can be postponed." External credit can be provided by private actors and by public authorities. External credit can be provided in the form of sovereign debt, corporate bonds, bank lending, and foreign equity purchases.

Financial power as such inheres to the national economy as a whole. That is, financial power does not inhere solely in ability of the government to borrow cheaply from the rest of the world, but in the ability of the economy as a whole to borrow cheaply from the rest of the world in large volumes and for extended periods. Thus, when we speak of American financial power, we are not speaking narrowly about the U.S. government's ability to finance a budget deficit by selling bonds to China (or Japan). Nor are we restricting our attention to monetary power; the benefits that accrue to the U.S. government from the dollar's role as the world's primary reserve currency. We are talking more broadly about the ability of all U.S. residents to sell financial assets, such as mortgage-backed securities, corporate bonds, stocks, bank deposits, as well as government bonds, to foreigners. Financial power is thus the ability to escape the "crowding out" constraint: when government borrowing increases, foreign capital rushes in to fill the gap between the increased demand for and an unchanged domestic supply of savings. The greater the ability to draw on external credit – the more willing foreign residents are to lend to domestic borrowers – the longer the country can delay implementing the policy changes necessary to reduce the gap between national income and national expenditures.

America's financial power derives from the interaction between country-level attributes and its location in the network structure of the international financial system. At the country level, "confidence" is the key factor (Chey 2012; Helleiner 2008). Confidence is fundamentally a function of credit risk and liquidity risk. Credit risk is the probability that a borrower will default. The probability of default in turn is a function of the underlying strength of the economy, which shapes the health of the corporate sector and thus the likelihood of default on corporate bonds. Default risk is a function of government reputation that shapes the probability of a sovereign default. Default risk is a function of the stability of the banking system. On all of these dimensions, the U.S. financial system scores high in absolute and relative terms: the risk of default is extremely low, lower in the United States than in all other countries. Liquidity risk is largely a function of the size of capital markets. Many countries offer sound investment opportunities; but most markets are relatively small. The United States, in contrast, has the largest and most active capital markets in the world. The liquidity of these markets generally enables holders of dollar-denominated assets of all kinds to liquidate their holdings quickly and at low cost. Country-level characteristics combine to make the U.S. financial system a market in which credit risk and liquidity risk are very low.

Country-level characteristics are reinforced by the network structure of the international financial system (Helleiner 2008; Oatley et al. 2013). The United States stands at the center of the global financial network. The United States attracts financial assets in larger amounts from more countries than any other national financial system in the world. And the difference between the United States and other countries is not linear; the United States is twice as central as the second most central system (the United Kingdom), four times more central than the third most central countries (Germany and Luxembourg), and orders of magnitude more central than the tenth most central countries.

America's central location in the global financial network generates positive feedback that encourages foreign capital to flow to the United States. The probability that the United States attracts foreign capital is a positive function of the amount of foreign capital it has attracted. The willingness of foreign investors to acquire additional dollar-denominated assets is a positive function of the volume of dollar-denominated assets foreigners hold. This dynamic contrasts sharply with the capital market dynamics that apply to other countries, where the volume of capital inflows is typically a negative function of current debt levels. In a sense, then, the United States has financial power because it has financial power to begin with.

Although existing literature highlights the factors that shape cross-national variation in potential or latent financial power, it offers little guidance on how to measure realized financial power. What I mean is that scholars agree that the depth and openness of American capital markets as well as America's central network location give the United States far greater financial power than any other country. As a consequence, we know that the United States has the potential to finance a larger current account or balance of payments deficit for a longer period and at lower cost than most other economies. Yet, the literature does not offer a time-varying measure that captures the degree to which the United States exploits this potential power and it has yet to identify the conditions under which the United States does so. Thus, if we wish to understand how financial power transforms buildups into booms, we need to fill these two gaps in our understanding of financial power.

I measure the degree to which the United States exploits its financial power by constructing a time series of the concentration of net cross-border capital flows between 1970 and 2008. To measure the concentration of cross-border capital flows, I calculated a Gini coefficient for the ten largest national current account deficits in each year. The ten largest deficits each year account for between 60 and 75 percent of the total annual global imbalance. I focus on the ten largest rather than all because in the more inclusive measures differences in GDP between the largest and smallest economies drive the result. The index begins in

1970 because this is the earliest year for which IMF data provide reasonable coverage, although coverage between 1970 and 1975 is sparse. This Gini coefficient rises toward unity as cross-border capital flows become heavily concentrated in a single country and falls toward zero when capital flows are more evenly distributed across the ten countries with the largest current account deficits. Over the whole period, the cross-national distribution of net capital flows has ranged from a low of 0.3 to a high of 0.85.

The cross-national distribution of net capital flows is highly correlated with the U.S. demand for foreign capital. Figure 4.5 plots the U.S. current account deficit – a measure of U.S. demand for foreign capital – against the cross-national distribution of net capital flows. The plot clearly indicates a strong positive relationship between U.S. current account deficits and the concentration of net cross-border capital flows. When the U.S. demand for foreign capital rises, it attracts an increasing share of net cross-border capital flows. When U.S. demand for foreign capital falls, net capital flows are more evenly distributed across the world's deficit countries. At one extreme, large U.S. current account deficits are associated with a Gini coefficient of 0.82. At the other end, small U.S. current account deficits are associated with Gini coefficients that range between 0.3 and 0.5. The concentration index thus offers a time-varying measure of America's financial power: when the American demand for

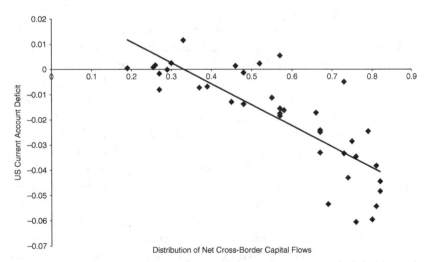

FIGURE 4.5. Current Account Deficits and the Concentration of Global Capital Flows.

TABLE 4.3. *Budget Deficits, Private Investment,*
and Capital Flows

Deficit	0.005
	(0.01)
Deficit × Buildup	−0.06***
	(0.02)
Private Investment	4.55*
	(2.35)
Private Investment × Buildup	0.33
	(0.34)
Buildup	−0.01
	(0.03)
Lagged Dependent Variable	0.03
	(0.15)
Constant	0.004
	(0.02)
Observations	37
F Statistic	5.21
Probability > F	0.001
Adjusted R²	0.41

Dependent variable is one-period change in concentration
of global capital flows.
***Significant at 0.99; **significant at 0.95; *significant at
0.90.

foreign capital rises, the United States attracts an increasing share of net
cross-border capital flows.

This concentration index allows us to identify the conditions under
which the United States exploits its financial power. Our expectation is
that variation in America's demand for foreign capital will be driven by
variation in budget deficits resulting from military buildups and by variation in private investment. Table 4.3 reports the results of an analysis
in which the one-period change in the concentration index is regressed
against the one-period change in the budget deficit and the one-period
change in private investment, with each variable conditioned on the presence or absence of a military buildup. The findings indicate that during
military buildups, changes in the budget deficit are significantly related
to changes in the concentration index, but in other periods, the budget
deficit is not related systematically to the concentration index. Thus, the
United States attracts additional foreign capital when it must pay for
unexpectedly large defense expenditures. In other periods, when military
spending has not increased sharply, variation in the concentration index

is responsive to changes in private investment: as private investment rises, the concentration index increases. The two relationships thus highlight the same core phenomenon: financial power. The American economy satisfied an increased demand for savings by attracting a larger share of cross-border capital flows.

Financial Power and Crowding Out

America's ability to attract foreign capital ensures that an increase in U.S. government borrowing to pay for increased military spending doesn't crowd out private investment and private consumption. As Greta Krippner has noted, American "policymakers discovered ... that they lived in a world in which capital was available in a potentially limitless supply. Access to global financial markets would allow the state to defer indefinitely the difficult political choices [as it struggled] to allocate scarce capital between competing social priorities" (Krippner 2011: 101–102).

We find evidence that postwar military buildups have not crowded out investment or private consumption using standard regression analysis. I regressed the one-period change in total private investment as a share of GDP against the one-period change in the budget deficit, controlling for change in interest rates and the change in private consumption. With the exception of the interest rate, all variables are standardized by GDP. I estimated versions of the model that employ the contemporaneous deficit as well as a one-period lag. I estimated the same specifications against private consumption expenditures. Because our concern here is with whether buildup-induced deficits have crowded out investment or private consumption, I restrict the sample to the set of years characterized by military buildups. This reduces the number of observations from forty-seven to twenty-three. Table 4.4 presents the results.

The four models convey a consistent message. The changes in the federal government budget deficit brought about by postwar military buildups have not been significantly related to negative changes in private investment or consumption. The contemporaneous specification indicates the absence of a systematic relationship between buildup-induced budget deficits and private investment. The lagged specification returned a statistically significant negative coefficient for change in deficit. This suggests that private investment's share of GDP rises during economic booms sparked by military buildups, even as the budget deficit widens. This finding suggests that the fiscal stimulus imparted by the buildup is

TABLE 4.4. *The Impact of Budget Deficits on Private Investment and Consumption During Booms*

	Private Investment		Private Consumption	
	Lagged Deficit	Deficit	Lagged Deficit	Deficit
Budget Deficit	−0.003**	0.001	0.001	0.001
	(0.001)	(0.001)	(0.001)	(0.001)
Prime Rate	0.001	0.001	−0.002**	−0.003**
	(0.001)	(0.001)	(0.001)	(0.001)
Private Consumption	−0.17	−0.37		
	(0.22)	(0.26)		
Private Investment			−0.13	−0.24
			(0.22)	(0.19)
Lagged Dependent	0.42***	0.14	−0.08	−0.11
Variable	(0.18)	(0.23)	(0.15)	(0.14)
Observations	23	23	23	23
F statistic	7.25	3.55	6.28	6.86
Probability > F	0.001	0.03	0.002	0.002
Adjusted R^2	0.53	0.32	0.49	0.52

Dependent variable is one-period change in private investment or consumption.
***Significant at 0.99; **significant at 0.95; *significant at 0.90.

amplified by the private sector as foreign capital allows for increased investment.

The results indicate no systematic relationship between changes in the budget deficit and changes in consumption during these economic booms. Changes in consumption expenditures during buildup-induced booms have been sensitive to changes in interest rates. As we would expect, consumption rises as lending rates fall over the course of the boom. The budget deficits that have resulted from postwar buildups have not crowded out either private investment or private consumption.

America's financial power thus allows the U.S. government to increase military spending sharply in response to foreign military challenges without needing to resolve political conflict over how to pay for it. Because the United States can import capital in large volumes at low cost for extended periods, policymakers face little diffuse market pressure to encourage agreement. And the ease with which the United States attracts foreign capital implies that the private sector does not face higher borrowing costs and thus has little reason to pressure the government to balance the budget. Financial power thereby enables the U.S. government to increase military spending without having to cut social welfare programs, without having to reduce private consumption, and without having to reduce private sector investment.

Conclusion

Deficit-financed military buildups have profoundly shaped America's postwar economic performance. On the one hand, postwar military buildups have driven macroeconomic performance. As we have seen, every deficit-financed military buildup has given rise to an extended period of robust economic growth, and three-quarters of all postwar booms have been triggered by these unexpected military buildups. The buildups trigger booms because they have been unexpected, because they have been pro-cyclical, and because they have been persistent. And though these booms have delivered apparent benefits in the form of extended periods of low and falling unemployment and rising per capita incomes, the booms also have had costs. The need to finance large and persistent budget deficits pushes interests up to attract capital into the American economy from abroad. Capital inflows trigger a sharp appreciation of the dollar. The combination of increased demand for imports and the overvalued dollar widen the current account deficit substantially. Deficit-financed buildups thus generate booms, but contribute also to large dollar appreciations and external imbalances.

Military buildups have had this economic impact because of U.S. financial power. America's location at the center of the global financial system, a position that rests on global confidence in American assets and the network dynamics of global finance, enables the United States to attract foreign capital in large volumes, at low rates, for extended periods. The United States has exploited this financial power whenever it has embarked upon a sustained increase in defense spending. During the Vietnam War, the Johnson administration pressured Germany and Japan to accumulate more dollars as foreign exchange reserves than they would have held in the absence of such pressure. Since 1975, capital markets have intermediated the flow of capital into the American economy as foreigners developed a very healthy appetite for dollar-denominated assets.

Because the United States attracts foreign capital so easily, the increased government borrowing that has been the consequence of postwar military buildups does not crowd out private investment in the American economy. Indeed, the results from the statistical analysis hint at a powerful positive feedback process at work. Budget deficits spark investment, and rising investment generates optimistic expectations about the future that encourages additional private investment. Rather than observing a crowding out phenomenon, financial power has generated a dynamic of crowding in. America's financial power thus allows the American economy to benefit from the dual impact of a sustained pro-cyclical fiscal expansion and an increase in private investment. The combination has unfailingly produced economic booms – extended episodes of rising prosperity.

A singular focus on aggregate prosperity, however, obscures disparities that emerge over the course of each boom. On the one hand, large swathes of American manufacturing struggle as the dollar appreciates and import competition rises. Consequently, and perhaps somewhat ironically, important segments of American industry find themselves battling for survival in the midst of rising prosperity. Typically, this battle unfolds in the trade policy arena, where business pressures Congress and the executive branch for protection from foreign competition. On the other hand, the investment that drives the boom shifts into the more competitive areas of the American economy, which in the context of an overvalued exchange rate and rising imports are sectors that face little international competition, either because they rely heavily on highly skilled workers (human capital and technology intensive manufacturing and financial services) or because they are not internationally traded at all (real estate and non-traded services). The imbalanced growth characteristic of buildup-induced booms thus alters the structure of the American economy.

5

Deflecting the Costs of Adjustment

> U.S. trade policy ... ended up a weak and unwilling handmaiden to macroeconomics. It was forced into trying to do what macroeconomic policy could or would not do.
>
> J. David Richardson[1]

Buildup-driven booms have had a powerful impact on American foreign economic policy. In particular, they have caused the United States to use trade and exchange rate policy to try to pressure its largest trade partners to adjust their policies in order to narrow global imbalances. The United States has sought to deflect the costs of adjusting current account deficits the boom generates by manipulating its trade partner's economic and security dependence. The United States has pressured its partners to eliminate trade barriers, purchase more American products, revalue their currencies, and embrace more expansive monetary and fiscal policies. It has applied this pressure through bilateral talks and through multilateral negotiations in which it threatens to withdraw American security commitments and restrict access to the U.S. market unless governments agree to change policy. And though clearly all governments would always prefer that other states bear the costs associated with reducing global imbalances, the intensity of American pressure on its trade partners has been greatest in the midst of its economic booms.

American policymakers' efforts to deflect adjustment costs have occurred as a response to rising protectionism among manufacturing

[1] Richardson (1994: 630).

and in the halls of Congress that the boom generates. The strong dollar and rising imports generated by the buildup-induced boom place the American manufacturing industry under greater strain. As foreign competition intensifies at home and overseas, individual firms and the business associations that represent them begin to pressure Congress. The House and Senate hold hearings on America's declining competitiveness. Legislators hear testimony about how America's trade partners are cheating, using trade and exchange rate policy to give their producers an unfair advantage in global markets. Legislators introduce bills that threaten to restrict foreign access to the American market unless such cheating stops. Somewhat paradoxically, therefore, economic booms generate substantial protectionist activity within Congress. The White House responds to the building pressure in Congress by pushing America's trade partners to alter their trade, exchange rate, and macroeconomic policies.

This chapter develops this argument in two steps. I focus first on the emergence of protectionism in Congress. I illustrate first the pro-cyclical nature of protectionism, demonstrating that the private sector's demand for protection as well as protectionist legislation rises during buildup-induced booms and ebbs in other periods. I then present statistical models to demonstrate that this variation is a consequence of variation in the dollar and the trade deficit. I then turn my attention to the resulting efforts to pressure trade partners to change policies. We look in broad terms at the many ways in which the United States has sought to push the costs of adjustment onto the surplus economies. I then present the results of some statistical models to demonstrate that American attempts to deflect adjustment costs have come as responses to rising congressional protectionism. I conclude by highlighting the consequences of America's efforts to deflect adjustment costs. I argue that the policy achieves little in terms of reducing global imbalances, producing instead economic conflict between the United States and its trade partners and an environment conducive to the development of financial fragility.

The Pro-cyclicality of Postwar Protectionism

Postwar trade politics have exhibited a remarkable degree of pro-cyclicality, with protectionist sentiment rising during buildup-induced booms and declining as the economy moves into recession. This pro-cyclicality is evident in two indicators of American trade politics (Figure 5.1). One indicator tracks the number of antidumping petitions filed by American industry each year. This indicator is particularly useful because through

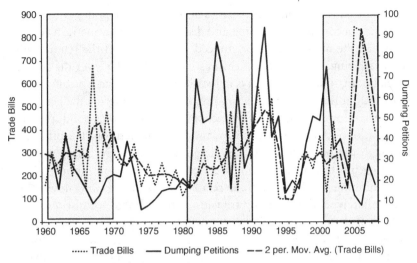

FIGURE 5.1. Booms and Protectionism.

much of the postwar era, industries have sought trade protection through administrative remedies rather than through legislated changes to tariff rates. Thus, tracking these petitions over time offers a direct indication of the number of industries willing to spend money in pursuit of protection. The second indicator is the number of trade-related bills introduced into the Senate and House each year, presented here as a two-year moving average. Though it is not a direct measure of protectionist activity, this index does illustrate the amount of attention that Congress devotes to trade policy. Together, the two indicators provide a macro perspective on the evolution of trade policy activity over the postwar period.

When juxtaposed against America's postwar booms, these indicators highlight the pro-cyclical nature of industry demands for protection and congressional trade policy activity. Notice first that our two indicators correlate fairly well with one another. This correlation strengthens if we lag the antidumping petitions one period and standardize trade-related bills by total congressional bills. This suggests that private sector activity and congressional activity move together over time. Indeed, one might suggest that the lagged correlation highlights a causal relationship: the amount of attention Congress directs toward trade is responsive to the amount of energy the private sector devotes to seeking protection. We will explore this relationship further in a moment.

For now, notice that both indicators track the economy's movement into and out of buildup-induced booms. Private sector antidumping petitions and the attention Congress devotes to trade policy rise when the American economy is booming and decline when the American economy is not in the midst of a boom. Indeed, the strength of the relationship is quite striking. One or both measures increase steadily over the course of each boom, though not always in lock step. The pattern is strongest in the Reagan boom, as both indicators trend up steadily across the period. The pattern is apparent though a bit weaker in the two other buildup-induced booms. In both of these instances, antidumping petitions fall off midway through the boom, while trade-related legislation rises sharply. Equally striking, protectionist activity declines as booms come to an end, with antidumping petitions and trade-related legislation trending down almost immediately as the economy transitions from boom to bust. Across the whole of the postwar period, American trade politics has thus exhibited a remarkable degree of pro-cyclicality, with industry demands for protection as well as congressional trade-related activity increasing over the course of economic booms and falling once booms come to an end.

Although antidumping petitions clearly represent firms' demands for protection, congressional activity during booms might reflect a greater propensity to liberalize trade rather than greater desire to restrict it. Indeed, the rise of antidumping petitions might be an industry response to increased trade liberalization enacted by the Congress. Thus, we need to supplement the trade legislation index with qualitative evidence on the overall orientation of congressional trade policy in these periods. This is particularly important in 1967 and 1968, as multilateral negotiations conducted within the General Agreement on Tariffs and Trade (the Kennedy Round) concluded in late May of 1967 and the authority Congress had delegated to the executive under the Trade Expansion Act (TEA) of 1962 expired in June of 1967. Hence, the spike of congressional activity in 1967 and 1968 might have focused on liberalizing trade – extending the TEA and enacting the Kennedy Round agreement.

Qualitative evidence suggests, however, that congressional activity was increasingly protectionist in this period. We see some evidence in the Johnson administration's rising concern about protectionist pressures in the summer and fall of 1967. Dean Rusk informed President Johnson in October 1967 that "current protectionist pressures pose a threat to our trade policy of an entirely different order of magnitude than we have had to face for many years. US import restrictions on steel and all forms of textiles, for example, would affect close to $3 billion, or about 11% of our total imports last year" (U.S. Department of State 1998: 372). Rusk requested Johnson's permission to allow key administration officials to testify before a hearing in the Senate Finance Committee that committee Chairman Russell Long had organized as a platform for the industries demanding protection. Rusk also proposed that the administration embark on a concerted effort to encourage export-oriented industries to establish an association that could provide an effective counter to protectionist interests. "We will have to urge leading American exporters, importers, financiers and shippers to be more visible and more vocal. The need for a major campaign of this kind is, I believe, very real" (Ibid).

We see broader evidence of the protectionist nature of congressional activity during this period by comparing the content of trade-related legislation between 1965 and 1968 to the content of trade-related bills introduced between 1960 and 1964. To make this comparison I assigned each trade-related bill proposed in each period a unique number. I then used a random number generator to produce a sample of fifty bills for each period. I then coded the content of each bill as protectionist, liberalizing, or other. During the first half of the decade, one-third of the sampled bills had a protectionist orientation – they called for the implementation of import quotas or other trade barriers. In the late 1960s, by contrast, approximately two-thirds of the sampled legislation was protectionist, proposing quotas, orderly marketing arrangements, and other trade-restricting measures. Moreover, protectionist legislation in the early 1960s focused on two issues: antidumping rules and oil import quotas. In contrast, protectionist legislation during the late 1960s targeted a wide set of industries. In the fall of 1967, for instance, Senate legislation proposed import quotas on about 11 percent of imports, including oil, meat, dairy, footwear, steel, and textiles, and these bills attracted broad support: ninety Senators sponsored at least one bill (Dryden 1995: 117).

The spike of congressional activity in the late 1980s exhibits similar characteristics. This period brought sustained pressure for protection by the nation's two largest manufacturing industries – automobiles and steel – and their associated downstream producers, as well as the affiliated unions. These mature capital-intensive industries were joined by manufacturing industries higher up the technology ladder, such as semiconductor chip producers (Schwab 1994: 53–54). As Richardson summarized, "Pressures to protect devastated U.S. industries and regions (especially the industrial "Rust Belt" in the mid-Atlantic and Midwest states) reached feverish intensity" in the middle of the decade (Richardson 1994: 630). Organized labor focused an increasing share of its resources on import quotas and domestic content measures that would protect unionized industry from imports (Schwab 1994: 55).

Congress responded to pressure by introducing legislation that threatened trade restrictions (Ahearn 1986; Ahearn and Reifman 1986, 1988). Congress focused particular attention on threats to restrict imports from surplus economies in retaliation for alleged unfair trade practices (Destler 1995: 83–84). In 1985, for instance, Congress considered the Gephardt–Bentsen–Rostenkowski Import Surcharge bill, which threatened to impose a 25 percent surcharge on imports from any country that had a large trade surplus with the United States and employed "unfair" trade policies (Schwab 1994: 69).

Congress focused its attention on the country with which the United States recorded its largest bilateral imbalance. During the 1980s, this put Japan at the center of congressional attention. Between 1985 and 1988, the U.S. bilateral trade deficit with Japan averaged $60 billion, slightly more than one-third of America's total trade deficit (Butler 1991). This large bilateral deficit with Japan became the central focus of congressional activity. Between 1985 and 1988, fifteen pieces of legislation were introduced into Congress that specifically threatened to restrict Japanese imports, demanded the removal of Japanese barriers to U.S. exports, or both. Some of the legislation was product specific; a 1985 bill, for instance, proposed an extension of import quotas on Japanese automobile imports. Other legislation had a much broader focus. Senator John Heinz (R-PA) sponsored a bill in 1985 that proposed a tariff surcharge on all imports from Japan. Other legislation sought to pressure the Reagan administration to pressure Japan. Bob Packwood (R-OR) proposed legislation that would "require the administration to respond to the unfair trade practices of Japan." Some legislation sought to increase the sale of American auto parts in the Japanese market; others sought increased sales of U.S. semiconductors. All of this congressional activity culminated in the 1988 enactment of the Omnibus Trade and Competitiveness Act (OTCA). The OTCA's key innovation lay in "Super 301," a mechanism by which Congress created a regularized process through which the executive branch was required to identify unfair trade practices of America's trade partners and then initiate bilateral negotiations to remove them.

During the 2000s, Congress focused on China. In mid-boom, America's bilateral deficit with China accounted for between one-quarter and one-third of America's total current account deficit. As a result, the American manufacturing industry targeted China in its effort to seek political action. A broad-based private sector coalition organized under the banner of the Fair Currency Alliance (FCA) and later renamed the China Currency Coalition (CCC) emerged in late 2003. The FCA/CCC organized the joint efforts of mature capital-intensive manufacturing industries, with a large concentration of members in steel, metalworking, and machine tools, as well as American labor unions that represented workers in these industries (Fair Currency Coalition 2010). The group launched a concerted campaign through which it pressured Congress and the administration to address the challenges posed by import competition. Much of this group's activities focused on China's currency policy. As a first strategy, the group filed a Section 301 petition in September 2004 requesting tariffs of approximately 27 percent on all imports from China in retaliation for what they believed to be China's undervalued currency. The Bush administration rejected the petition the very day it was filed. The group subsequently directed most of its energy toward Congress, where it sought legislation that would impose tariffs on imports from China unless China revalued its currency. Between 2003 and 2008, Congress considered approximately fifty such pieces of legislation (Hufbauer, Wong, and Sheth 2006).

America's buildup-induced booms have thus generated substantial protectionist pressure. The manufacturing industry faces stiffer competition as the dollar strengthens and imports rise. It responds to this competition by turning to Congress for relief. Congress has responded to industry pressure by devoting more attention to trade and by threatening to restrict foreign access to the U.S. market. Congressional attention has focused most heavily on those countries with which the United States runs its largest bilateral trade deficit. Germany and Japan received the greatest scrutiny during the 1960s, Japan was the center of attention during the 1980s, and China occupied this position in the 2000s. As a consequence of these developments, each boom generated substantial pressure from Congress on the White House to take steps to remove the unfair foreign practices that legislators saw as the cause of America's trade deficit.

Why Booms Generate Protectionism

The pro-cyclical character of America's postwar protectionism runs counter to conventional thinking. Existing research that explores the relationship between protectionism and the business cycle argues the converse proposition: protectionism should rise during recessions, when industry has substantial surplus capacity, and fall during expansions when domestic demand is strong (see, e.g., Bagwell and Staiger 2003; Bown and Crowley 2013; Cassing, McKeown, and Ochs 1986; Costinot 2009; Gallarotti 1985; Grilli 1988; McKeown 1984; Takacs 1981). One recent paper summarizes this consensus, "there seems to be universal agreement [among political economists] that protectionism is counter-cyclic" (Rose 2013: 31). Why does the American postwar experience defy conventional wisdom? Why do industry demands for protection as well as congressional protectionist legislation rise during those periods during which the national economy is enjoying sustained growth?

Postwar protectionism has been pro-cyclical because the benefits generated by postwar booms are unevenly distributed across sectors of the economy. In particular, many traded goods producers struggle in the face of intensified foreign competition during booms (Frieden 1991, 1997; Oatley 2010). As we saw in Chapter 4, deficit-financed military build-ups have strengthened the dollar and widened the trade deficit. These exchange rate and trade consequences of domestic macroeconomic imbalances disadvantage American manufacturers. At home, the strong dollar and rising imports erode domestic manufacturing firms' share of the U.S. market in many industries. Overseas, the strong dollar raises the price of American exports, thereby eroding American producers' shares of foreign markets. Thus, in the midst of an economic boom, large swathes of American manufacturing confront increased foreign competition at home and abroad. American manufacturers turn to the political system in search of relief, hoping that higher tariffs at home or fewer trade barriers abroad might offset their growing competitive disadvantage. And thus we observe the paradoxical pro-cyclical nature of American protectionism.

The systematic relationship between the real exchange rate, the current account, and protectionism is evident in a time series analysis of antidumping petition filings and congressional trade-related legislation for the period 1960–2008. The dependent variables in this analysis – antidumping petitions and congressional trade legislation – are the same measures discussed earlier. I measure one key independent variable – the dollar's real exchange rate – with the real effective exchange rate index created by Bruegel (Darvas 2012). Real exchange rate indices created by the Federal Reserve, as well as those available through international economic organizations, extend back only to 1973. The Bruegel index provides an additional thirteen years of coverage, thereby allowing me to extend the analysis back to 1960 and thus cover the entire period under investigation here. The Federal Reserve's index and the Bruegel index correlate at 0.94 across the thirty-nine years for which both exist, and Bruegel index values for the 1960s are consistent with export price indices for the decade reported in other research (see, e.g., Eichengreen 2000). I expect a positive coefficient on this variable. I measure my second key independent variable, the Trade Balance, with the current account balance as a share of GDP. I expect a negative coefficient. Because private industry demands for protection are likely to affect congressional trade policy activity, I include Antidumping Petitions in the model of trade legislation as a proxy for industry activity. As business mobilizes in search of protection, Congress should devote greater attention to trade policy. I thus expect antidumping petitions to have a positive relationship with congressional trade legislation.

I control for a variety of potentially confounding economic and political factors. I control for the business cycle with two variables: the unemployment rate and the real growth rate. I control for two characteristics of the partisan composition of government. I control for divided government, coding as 1 any year in which different parties control Congress and the executive branch. I also control for the party of the president; years in which a Democrat occupies the White House are coded 1. I also control for the interaction between these two configurations.

Because antidumping petitions is a count variable, a standard ordinary least squares analysis is inappropriate. And because the data for the dependent variable are overdispersed (variance is greater than the mean), I employ a negative binomial regression rather than Poisson regression. The Trade Legislation dependent variable is a continuous measure, and thus I estimate these models using ordinary least squares with a lagged dependent variable. The results are presented in Tables 5.1 and 5.2.

We look first at the results from the model of antidumping petitions (Table 5.1). The findings provide rather strong and consistent evidence for the proposition that private industry antidumping petition filings have been highly responsive to changes in the value of the dollar. The coefficient on *Real Exchange Rate* is statistically significant and appropriately signed. Dollar appreciations are followed by an increased number of antidumping petition filings and dollar depreciations are followed by a reduced number of petitions. The relationship is substantively important. A one standard deviation dollar appreciation is associated with six additional antidumping petition filings. Given that the average number of petitions filed each year is twenty-eight, then a relatively large appreciation – from one to two standard deviations – increases the number of antidumping petitions that industry files by between 25 and 50 percent. And given that the most substantial dollar appreciations have occurred during booms, this suggests that the rising demand for protection we observe during booms is driven by the manufacturing industry's response to competitiveness problems that result from a strong dollar.

TABLE 5.1. *The Dollar and Antidumping Petitions*

Lag Antidumping	0.01***
	0.04
Dollar Appreciation	0.04***
	0.004
Unemployment	0.02
	0.06
Current Account Balance	−3.46
	4.50
Growth Rate	7.48
	4.27
Divided Government	1.35**
	0.63
Party of the President	0.88
	0.66
Divided Government × Party of the President	−1.27*
	0.69
Observations	50
Probability>χ^2	0.0002

Dependent variable is the number of antidumping investigations filed each year.
***Significance at 0.99; **significance at 0.95; *significance at 0.90.

TABLE 5.2. *Industry Demands and Congressional Trade Bills*

Lag Trade Bills	−0.23*
	0.13
Antidumping Petitions	0.0003***
	0.0001
Current Account Balance	−0.48***
	0.14
Dollar Appreciation	0.0002
	0.0005
Unemployment	0.002
	0.002
Growth Rate	−0.05
	0.13
Divided Government	0.02***
	0.001
Party of the President	0.02***
	0.007
Observations	47
R^2	0.42
Probability>F	0.0002

Dependent variable is trade-related legislation bills as a share of all legislation.
***Significant at 0.99; **significant at 0.95; *significant at 0.90.

Only one of the political and economic control variables returned a statistically significant coefficient. *Divided Government* returned a significant positive coefficient, indicating that the number of antidumping petitions filed is greater during periods of divided government than during periods of unified government. The magnitude of the effect is large, with about ten additional petitions filed each year under divided government. *Party of the President* did not yield a significant coefficient. The interaction between these two political variables is weakly significant and carries a negative sign. This suggests that divided government is an important determinant of petition findings only when a Republican is in the White House. Under a Democratic administration, divided government has no significant impact on the demand for protection. One wonders if this interaction highlights a dynamic specific to the Reagan administration. More generally, this might suggest that industry is more likely to turn to administrative channels when a greater number of veto players make it more difficult to secure legislated action.

Only one of the economic control variables approached traditional levels of statistical significance. The estimated impact of *Growth Rate* was weakly significant. Yet, in contrast to conventional wisdom, the coefficient carries a positive sign, indicating that, controlling for other factors, the demand for protection is stronger during economic expansions than during recessions. This further reinforces our claim that postwar protectionism in the United States has been pro-cyclical, while the weakness of the relationship suggests that growth per se is a less systematic driver of protectionism than the relative price impact of the stronger dollar that has accompanied this growth. Neither *Unemployment* nor the *Current Account* approached conventional levels of statistical significance. Thus, it seems that the exchange rate plays a systematic role in driving variation in industry demands for protection over time, and to the extent that the business cycle has shaped the demand for protection its impact appears to be pro-cyclic.

The results from our models of congressional trade legislation are also consistent with our expectations. Variation in the attention that Congress devotes to trade is a function of industry demands for protection and the current account balance (Table 5.2). Private sector demands for protection, which I proxy with *Antidumping Petitions*, returns a positive and significant coefficient. Congressional attention to trade policy rises in line with and presumably as a response to industry demands for protection. The estimated size of the coefficient indicates that every one standard deviation increase in antidumping petitions increases trade legislation's share of the congressional agenda by approximately one percentage point. Given that the share of congressional bills accounted for by trade legislation never rises above 8 percent, this constitutes a fairly substantial shift within the effective range of the measure. Notice that *Dollar Appreciation* carries the expected sign but does not approach statistical significance. This suggests that the impact of the real exchange rate on trade politics flows through its impact on private industry demand, and private industry demand in turn drives congressional action.

The *Current Account* also returns a statistically significant negative relationship with trade legislation. As the current account balance deteriorates, Congress focuses more attention on trade politics. The magnitude of the relationship is substantial. A one standard deviation change in the current account balance alters the share of congressional attention dedicated to trade by approximately 1 percentage point. Although 1 percent may seem a small effect, trade policy accounts at most for only 8 percent of all legislation in any given year and on average accounts for less than 3 percent of all legislation. Hence a 1 percentage point change in share represents a meaningfully large change in this variable. For instance, a 4 percent deterioration of the current account, a shift in magnitude similar to that that occurred between 1981 and 1986 and 2001 to 2008, increases trade's share of the congressional agenda by 25 percent. The 2 percent deterioration, like that which occurred between 1965 and 1967, would be expected to increase trade's share by about 12 percent.

The two political control variables returned significant coefficients. The positive coefficient for *Divided Government* indicates that trade attracts 1 percentage point more of the congressional agenda when government is divided than when it is unified. The positive coefficient for *Party of the President* indicates that trade consumes more of the congressional agenda when a Democrat occupies the White House than when a Republican controls the executive branch. The interaction term never approached statistical significance, and thus I omitted it from the final specification. Neither measure of the economy's position in the business cycle returned a significant coefficient in any specification. This most likely reflects the high correlation between the current account balance and the business cycle. It might also suggest that congressional attention to trade responds more to lobbying by private industry than to macroeconomic conditions.

As an additional robustness check, I estimated models of congressional trade legislation with the dependent variable measured as first difference rather than level. The results were effectively identical: antidumping petitions returned a significant positive coefficient, current account balance a significant negative coefficient, and divided government and party of the president were both positive and significant. Neither growth nor unemployment was statistically significant. Like the model of antidumping petitions, therefore, the model of congressional activity provides little indication that congressional trade policy activity varies directly as a function of the economy's position in the business cycle. Instead, the pro-cyclicality has been driven by the currency and trade consequences of postwar booms.

The pro-cyclical nature of postwar protectionism thus appears to have been a consequence of the manufacturing industry's response to the impact of budget deficits on the dollar and the trade balance. The overvalued dollar and the surge of imports that result from the deficit-driven boom generate intensified foreign competition for the American manufacturing industry. Industry responds to this competition by turning to the political system for relief. Industry increases the number of antidumping petitions that it files and it increases the pressure it applies on legislators. As industry demands enter Congress, they combine with growing congressional concern about widening American trade deficits to increase the amount of attention directed toward trade policy. The result is a sharp increase in protectionist legislation that threatens to restrict foreign access to the U.S. market and that demands foreign removal of trade barriers that restrict American exports.

The Politics of Deflection

The White House has responded to protectionism in Congress by initiating bilateral and multilateral negotiations through which it has pressured its trade partners to make policy adjustments the United States believed would reduce the bilateral trade imbalance.

American policymakers have sought four types of policy adjustment. First, American policymakers have pressured surplus governments to increase direct purchases of American products. During the 1960s, the United States pursued this goal through offset agreements that it negotiated with the German government. These offset agreements committed Germany to purchase American military equipment in an amount sufficient to offset the impact that U.S. military spending in Germany had on the balance of payments. And although offset agreements began in 1961, the Johnson administration placed increasing importance upon them as it escalated America's involvement in Vietnam (Gavin 2004; Zimmermann 1996, 2002). The Reagan administration exerted similar pressure on the Japanese government from the mid-1980s. Rather than encourage government purchases of military equipment, the Reagan administration pushed for civilian procurement. The Japanese government responded to the pressure by encouraging public and private sector entities to purchase American products: Nippon Telephone and Telegraph, for instance, purchased several Cray Supercomputers, as did Honda and Nissan; Japan Airlines and All Nippon Airways placed large orders for commercial aircraft with Boeing. The Bush administration exerted similar pressure on the Chinese government during the 2000s, and China responded much like Japan had in the 1980s. More than 200 Chinese executives from state-owned as well as private firms accompanied Vice-Premier Wu Yi on an April 2006 visit to the United States. During their visit, the delegation signed contracts totaling more than $18 billion, the largest of which was an agreement to purchase eighty Boeing-737 aircraft for state-owned China Airlines.

American policymakers have also pressured surplus states to remove trade barriers. Administrations pursued this goal through multilateral and bilateral channels. Multilaterally, American policymakers attached great significance to trade negotiations within the General Agreement on Tariffs and Trade. The Johnson administration viewed the Kennedy Round as an important measure that would ensure that the newly operative European customs union would be open to U.S. goods (Zeiler 1992). The Reagan administration used the Uruguay Round to liberalize trade in services and agriculture as well as to create global rules to protect intellectual property. All three initiatives promised to create new export opportunities for highly competitive American industries.

American policymakers have relied on bilateral talks to exert particular pressure on the countries with which the United States runs large bilateral deficits. The United States conducted an extensive series of negotiations with Japan during the mid-1980s. The 1984 yen/dollar agreement opened the Japanese financial sector to American participation (Krippner 2011). The Market-Oriented Sector Selective talks initiated in 1985 sought to open the Japanese market for telecommunications, electronics, medical equipment and pharmaceuticals, and auto parts for U.S. firms. A 1986 semiconductor agreement appeared to promise American chip manufacturers a 10 percent share of the Japanese market. In the early 2000s, the Bush administration initiated bilateral talks with China within the Joint Commission on Commerce and Trade and the Strategic Economic Dialogue to pressure the Chinese government to strengthen the protection of intellectual property rights and to open its financial sector to U.S. firms. Bilateral talks had the advantage of not requiring American concessions; administration officials could negotiate on the premise that policies in place provided unfair competitive advantages and as such were inconsistent with the spirit of the global trade regime (if not always with the letter of the law) and thus should be removed.

American policymakers have also pressured surplus economies to revalue their currencies. The Johnson administration believed that the German mark was undervalued by at least 10 percent, and pushed the German government to revalue (U.S. Department of State 1998, Doc 199). The Reagan administration initiated a multilateral currency realignment in September 1985 – the Plaza Accord – that gradually revalued the yen and mark against the dollar. Indeed, concern with the impact of undervalued currencies on the U.S. trade balance in this period led Congress to include in the 1988 Omnibus Trade Act the requirement that the U.S. Treasury identify governments that manipulate their currencies to gain an unfair commercial advantage and initiate negotiations with these countries to end the manipulation. Finally, the Bush administration steadily pressured China to revalue the renminbi between 2002 and 2008 (Hufbauer, Wong, and Sheth 2006). Congress reinforced the Bush administration's efforts by holding its feet to the fire on the release of each issue of the Treasury Department's biannual *Report on Currency Manipulators*.

Finally, the United States has pressured its largest trade partners to adopt expansionary monetary and fiscal policies. Emphasis on macroeconomic expansion by the surplus economies received greatest attention during the second Reagan administration (Funabashi 1988; Webb 1991). Here, the administration followed the exchange rate realignment agreed in the Plaza Accord with sustained pressure on Germany and Japan to reduce interest rates, cut taxes, and increase government expenditures to boost domestic demand and thus narrow their surpluses. Baker agreed that the United States would raise taxes or cut expenditures to reduce the American budget deficit. Monetary policy coordination was a central component of pegged exchange rates under Bretton Woods; German money supply had to expand as a consequence of foreign exchange market intervention undertaken to sustain the mark's peg to the dollar. China's macroeconomic policy received less attention. Instead, the Bush administration emphasized China's high savings rate, which it attributed to demographics and an underdeveloped financial system as well as to the government's exchange rate and monetary policy (Council of Economic Advisors 2006). They thus pressured China to increase domestic consumption and reduce foreign exchange market intervention.

The United States encouraged governments in Germany, Japan, and China to change policy by manipulating their trade and security dependence on the United States. In negotiations with Japan and China, policymakers manipulated their dependence on the U.S. market. To do so, policymakers made it clear that failure to produce substantive results in bilateral talks would cause Congress to restrict sharply their access to the U.S. market (Cao et al. 2011). The Reagan administration relied heavily on Section 301 of the Trade Act of 1974, which obligated the executive branch to take all appropriate action, including retaliatory trade barriers, to remove unreasonable or discriminatory barriers to American exports (Destler 1991, 2005). Between 1985 and 1989, the administration initiated thirty-one such investigations and threatened to initiate an additional twenty-three. This represented a 50 percent increase in the frequency of actual investigations, and a fourfold increase in the number of threatened investigations relative to the prior decade (Bayard and Elliott 1994: 60–61). With China, Treasury Department officials engaged in sustained but quieter pressure through discussions with Chinese officials while Congress introduced bills that threatened to impose a 20 percent tariff on goods entering from China,

The Johnson administration manipulated German and Japanese dependence on the American security guarantee. The administration told Germany and Japan that America's balance of payments problems would force reductions of the number of U.S. troops stationed in their countries. Secretary of Defense Robert McNamara was the strongest proponent of this approach within the administration, and important congressional leaders such as Mike Mansfield were eager to move in this direction. Germany responded to American concerns by accepting a second Offset Agreement under which they committed to purchase $675 million of U.S. military equipment (Zimmermann 1996: 339–340). The administration pursued a very similar line toward Japan from 1966 on, pressing Japan to procure as much as $1 billion in U.S. military equipment to offset most of the bilateral trade imbalance, and to cover the remaining imbalance by purchasing U.S. government debt (U.S. Department of State 2006, Docs 72, 93, 95).

Correlates of Deflection

The historical evidence therefore suggests that the White House responded to protectionism in Congress by pressing America's largest trade partners to take steps to reduce their trade surpluses. The historical evidence leaves considerable uncertainty regarding two important issues, however. First, the descriptive history of American efforts to get surplus economies to adjust says little about variation in the intensity of this pressure or the extent to which pressure emerges in response to Congress. We can reduce both uncertainties by estimating a time series model of U.S. efforts to deflect adjustment costs onto the surplus economies.

My measure of executive branch pressure on surplus economies comes from sanctions data generated by the Threat and Imposition of Economic Sanctions (TIES) project (Morgan et al. 2013). The TIES data disaggregate trade sanctions by their intended purpose. I rely on what they call "Trade Practices: sanctions that the US threatened or imposed in order to compel the target state to alter a trade practice or to punish a target state for engaging in a particular practice. Examples may include sanctions to end protectionist measures, tariffs, trade restrictions, or devaluations" (Morgan et al. 2013: 4). This definition corresponds closely to the four policy changes the United States has sought in bilateral negotiations with its trade partners. Moreover, the TIES data count not only those sanctions that were implemented, but also those that were threatened but not implemented. These data cover the period 1974–2005.

My primary independent variables are *Antidumping Petitions* and *Congressional Trade Bills*. I expect that the number of trade sanctions the executive branch imposes each year will be a positive function of private sector demands for protection, which I proxy with *Antidumping Petitions* and of congressional trade policy activity, which I measure using the index of trade legislation employed in the previous section. I also control for the current account balance and the real effective exchange rate. Finally, as I did in the previous models, I control for the macroeconomic environment with unemployment and real economic growth rates. And because the dependent variable is a count of sanctions, I estimate a negative binomial regression. The results are reported in Table 5.3.

The estimates indicate that U.S. reliance on sanctions to try to compel the removal of foreign trade barriers has been highly responsive to protectionist sentiment in industry and Congress. Our measures of industry demands for protection and congressional trade policy activity return statistically and substantively significant coefficients. The positive

TABLE 5.3. *Deflecting Adjustment Costs*

	1974–2008	1974–2000
Lag Trade Sanctions	−0.07***	0.05**
	0.03	0.02
Antidumping Petitions	0.03***	0.03***
	0.01	0.01
Trade Bills	23.70**	22.72**
	11.13	9.37
Dollar Appreciation	0.06*	0.02
	0.03	0.03
Unemployment	−0.37*	−0.12
	0.21	0.22
Current Account Balance	79.82***	18.04
	18.78	36.13
Observations	35	27
Probability >F	0.0001	0.002

Dependent variable is the number of trade sanctions threatened and implemented each year.
***Significant at 0.99; **significant at 0.95; *significant at 0.90.

coefficients indicate trade sanctions rise in line with the number of anti-dumping petitions and with the amount of attention Congress devotes to trade. The substantive effects are large – every one unit increase in trade's share of the congressional agenda increases the number of sanctions by 1.25, and each one unit change in antidumping petitions alters the number of sanctions by 1.03. Thus, the executive's reliance on trade sanctions to pressure surplus economies to bear the adjustment costs has been highly responsive to demands for protection by private industry and Congress.

In contrast, economic conditions appear to have had a much weaker direct relationship to efforts to deflect adjustment. The dollar and unemployment are both marginally significant and suggest that administrations rely more heavily on sanctions as the dollar appreciates and unemployment falls. This finding is consistent with our observation of the pro-cyclical character of American protectionism. The current account balance returns a highly significant positive coefficient, suggesting that the United States imposes sanctions more frequently when the current account is strong than when the current account is weak.

The results from model 2, however, suggest that the statistical significance of the economic variables is driven by the inclusion of the Bush administration in the sample, a period characterized by the largest current account deficit and the fewest sanctions. If these five years are excluded from the sample, none of the economic variables approach conventional levels of statistical significance, though the estimated effect of private industry demands and congressional activity change very little. Model 3 thus interacts the current account balance with the Bush administration. Private industry demands for protection and congressional trade bills are significantly related to the executive's use of trade sanctions across the entire time period, while the measures of macroeconomic conditions fail to return statistically significant coefficients. The Bush administration thus was less inclined than Reagan to threaten trade sanctions in order to induce policy adjustments abroad.

The United States has thus responded to rising protectionism at home by trying to encourage policy adjustment overseas. Administration officials have initiated bilateral and multilateral negotiations through which they encouraged governments to purchase American products, remove trade barriers, revalue their currencies, and implement expansionary fiscal and monetary policies. Administration policymakers have pursued these policy changes by threatening to restrict surplus economies' access to the American market.

Conclusion

The United States has responded to the buildup-induced macroeconomic imbalances by trying to deflect the costs of adjustment onto large surplus economies. The United States has used bilateral and multilateral negotiations to encourage its trade partners to procure American products, remove trade barriers, revalue their currencies, and embrace a more expansionary macroeconomic policy mix. To encourage its trade partners to implement these policy adjustments, the United States has manipulated aspects of their dependence on America. The Reagan and Bush administrations encouraged Japan and China to adjust by threatening to restrict their access to the American market, the most important export destination for both economies. The Johnson administration encouraged Germany and Japan to adjust their economic policies by threatening to reduce the number of U.S. troops stationed in each country.

The degree to which the United States sought to deflect the costs of adjustment onto its trade partners was a function of the strength of protectionist sentiment within Congress. And the rise of protectionist sentiment in Congress was in turn driven by the reaction of manufacturing industry to a strengthening dollar and rising imports. As these dual consequences of the buildup-induced boom intensified foreign competition, American producers sought protection. They initiated antidumping investigations and they lobbied Congress. Legislators responded by introducing legislation that obligated the executive branch to be a more assertive advocate for and defender of American firms in global markets. Through this process Congress forced the White House to identify unfair trade policies abroad and negotiate their removal under the threat of sanction.

America's effort to deflect the costs of adjustment on to its trade partners failed to achieve its primary economic objective. American pressure did secure concessions from the surplus states. Germany purchased more military equipment, and Japan removed some non-tariff barriers. Germany, Japan, and China all revalued their currencies, and Japan and Germany accepted a more expansionary macroeconomic policy mix than they would have enacted in the absence of American pressure. Yet, these concessions had limited impact on the trade imbalances they were intended to adjust. The simplest indicator of this limited impact lies in the fact that the U.S. trade balance deteriorated continuously through each buildup-induced boom and improved only as booms turned to bust. While American efforts to deflect the costs of adjustment thus brought about policy changes, these efforts achieved relatively little adjustment.

Rather than bring about current account adjustment, American efforts to deflect adjustment had two unintended negative consequences. First, pressure on the surplus economies generated resentment and political conflict. America's trade partners felt, and quite rightly so, that the United States was forcing them to bear the costs of correcting problems made in America. America's trade partners thus resisted the pressure as best they could and criticized U.S. policy, especially fiscal policy. Second, because deflection was not especially productive, it delayed the onset of adjustment at home. And this delay wound up being extraordinarily costly. For by delaying the onset of adjustment at home by trying to force adjustment abroad, the United States allowed monetary and financial fragilities to develop at the center of the global economy.

6

The Financial Consequences of America's Postwar Booms

> The tendency to transform doing well into a speculative investment boom is the basic instability in a capitalist economy.
>
> Hyman Minsky[1]

Postwar economic booms triggered by military buildups have been the underlying cause of every major episode of financial and monetary instability the United States has experienced since World War II. The United States has suffered two major system-wide banking crises since 1945. The first struck hardest in 1988. Yet, the crisis, which was centered in savings and loan (S&L) institutions, evolved over a longer period. Between 1985 and 1992 approximately half of the existing S&Ls – more than 1,500 in number – were closed due to insolvency. At the time, the S&L crisis was the largest systemic banking crisis to occur in the American economy since the Great Depression. The second systemic banking crisis occurred in 2008. In this episode, five of the largest U.S. investment banks were closed or restructured, commercial banks that collectively held more than 15 percent of all commercial bank assets failed, and the major U.S. banking groups that didn't fail survived only by virtue of a massive injection of public funds. The United States has also suffered one episode of monetary instability. Beginning in early 1968, the United States experienced a run on the dollar, characterized by speculative attacks on the dollar's peg to gold of varying intensity, that persisted through early 1973 and forced the U.S. government to end the convertibility of the dollar into gold and

[1] Minsky (1977: 24).

destroyed the international monetary system as a consequence. As is evident, each of these three episodes occurred late in the economic boom, triggered by a major military buildup.

These episodes of financial and monetary instability arose from the booms generated by deficit-financed military buildups. The two banking crises occurred as the last step in a three-stage process. In the first stage, pro-cyclical fiscal policy imparted by the military buildup and the resulting economic boom combined with extremely large capital inflows to spark a credit boom. In the second stage, the credit boom interacted with a real exchange rate appreciation to generate an asset bubble centered in real estate. Housing prices rose, investment shifted into real estate, and bank balance sheets became increasingly concentrated on assets whose values were tied directly to real estate. In the third stage, the real estate bubble deflated, weakening bank balance sheets throughout the mortgage finance industry and thereby generating a systemic banking crisis.

The speculative attack on the dollar was the product of a two-stage sequence. In the first stage, the military buildup yielded an expansionary macroeconomic policy mix that was inconsistent with the government's commitment to the dollar's fixed exchange rate. In the second stage, speculators recognized the inevitability of a devaluation given the inconsistency between policy and the peg, and liquidated their dollar-denominated holdings to avoid the anticipated loss. In short, America's postwar banking and currency crises have emerged as the financial and monetary consequences of the large and persistent macroeconomic imbalances generated by deficit-financed military buildups.

I develop this argument in the following way. I focus first on the causal link between military buildups and banking crises. To do so, I draw on existing research that has explored the causes of postwar banking crises in other industrial and emerging market economies to identify those conditions that have generated banking crises elsewhere. I then demonstrate that the conditions that generated America's two postwar banking crises match the conditions that have generated banking crises elsewhere almost exactly. The only difference is in the source of the initial shock. In the U.S. case, the initial shock comes in both instances from military buildups. I then turn my attention to currency crises. I employ first-generation models of speculative attacks to generate theoretical expectations about why the expansionary macroeconomic policy generated by the military buildup was inconsistent with the dollar's peg to gold. I then demonstrate how in practice the expansionary macroeconomic policy triggered speculative attacks against the dollar that forced American policymakers to suspend convertibility and abandon the fixed exchange rate.

The conclusion summarizes the evidence and explains why a similar policy choice – the decision to deficit finance a military buildup rather than pay for the power from current income – generated a currency crisis in one instance and real estate bubbles and banking crises in two others. The different consequences, I argue, were a result of the different international monetary systems within which the imbalances emerged. The Vietnam War boom emerged in the context of the Bretton Woods System's fixed exchange rates and limited capital mobility, while the two subsequent booms occurred in the context of floating exchange rates and internationally mobile capital.

Banking Crises: Theoretical Considerations

Economists have embraced an event study approach to banking crises. Researchers working within this tradition first identify events – banking crises, currency crises – and then examine the behavior of macroeconomic and financial aggregates in the window that surrounds them (Claessens et al. 2013; Claessens and Kose 2013; Dell'Ariccia et al. 2013; Kaminsky and Reinhart 1999; Reinhart and Rogoff 2008a, 2008b). Although this inductive approach has yet to generate strong theory, it has produced consensus about the macroeconomic and financial conditions from which postwar banking crises across the globe have emerged. What is perhaps most striking about this work is how similar the processes are across time and space. In broad terms, this research finds that banking crises have occurred as the last of a three-stage dynamic. We look at each stage in turn.

In the first stage, large and sustained macroeconomic imbalances generate credit booms. A credit boom is a period during which credit extended to the private sector grows above its trend rate (Claessens and Kose 2013; Dell'Ariccia et al. 2013, 13; Mendoza and Terrones 2008; Terrones 2004). In the postwar era, credit booms have emerged in the context of macroeconomic environments with three dominant characteristics (see, e.g., Alesina, Campante, and Tabellini 2008; Gavin and Perrotti 1997; Kaminsky, Reinhart, and Végh 2005; Talvi and Vegh 2005). First, credit booms have emerged in the midst of ongoing and fairly robust economic expansions (Dell'Arricia et al. 2013: 13). A sustained economic expansion likely contributes to credit booms by shaping investor expectations;

a record of strong growth across multiple years encourages investors to become more optimistic about the future. Optimism about the future increases the willingness to invest in new projects, thereby increasing the demand for credit.

Second, credit booms have emerged in the context of "capital flow bonanzas." A capital flow bonanza is a sustained period of above-trend capital inflows. Researchers have identified the correlation between capital flow bonanzas and credit booms from two directions. One line of research identifies capital flow bonanzas using a threshold approach (capital inflows exceeding the 20th percentile for a given country) and then correlate these episodes with credit booms (Kaminsky and Reinhart 1999; Reinhart and Reinhart 2009). Other research has identified credit booms and then explored the behavior of capital flows in these episodes (Dell'Ariccia et al. 2013; Mendoza and Terrones 2008). Jointly, this work finds that during the typical capital flow bonanza capital inflows increase from 2.3 to 3.1 percent of gross domestic product (GDP). Bonanzas persist for between two and four years on average, with a few lasting as long as six years. Capital flow bonanzas trigger credit booms by providing funds that relax local constraints on credit growth. As a result, the capital inflows allow increasingly optimistic investors to borrow at low interest rates.

Finally, credit booms have emerged in the context of strongly pro-cyclical fiscal policy. Scholars have found that large budget deficits emerge in the context of ongoing economic expansions two or more years before the onset of a credit boom (see, e.g., Alesina, Campante, and Tabellini 2008; Gavin and Perrotti 1997; Kaminsky, Reinhart, and Végh 2005; Talvi and Vegh 2005). Rather than treat these three macroeconomic factors as independent variables, economists view them as a configuration of mutually reinforcing conditions. Under this "when it rains it pours" logic, positive feedback between growth, capital flow bonanzas, and fiscal policy accelerates and extends the economic expansion as well as the growth of credit. Robust growth attracts foreign capital that further stimulates GDP growth, while pro-cyclical fiscal policy further stimulates demand, which attracts additional capital inflows. As this positive feedback evolves over time, a credit boom emerges as increasingly optimistic investors draw on abundant capital inflows to invest, and the apparent high returns on investment induce additional capital inflows. And though this research finds that fiscal policy in industrialized countries is generally counter-cyclical, we have seen here that the specific case of U.S. fiscal policy has exhibited powerful pro-cyclical tendencies.

In the second stage, credit booms generate asset price bubbles. Asset price bubbles arise in real estate markets in particular (Bordo and Jeanne 2002; Gerdrup 2003; Reinhart and Reinhart 2009). In the eighteen industrialized countries that experienced a systemic banking crisis between 1970 and 2007, real estate prices rose by an average of 13 percent in the three years that preceded the crisis. In the five most severe crises that occurred in the industrialized world before 2008, housing prices rose by almost 20 percent in the three years before the onset of crisis. The Nordic country banking crises of the late 1980s and early 1990s followed this pattern. The Japanese banking crisis of the early 1990s followed this pattern. Research on a larger sample that incorporates middle-income countries as well as the industrialized countries suggests that a 1 percent increase of capital inflows is associated with a 10 percent increase in real estate prices (Aizenman and Jinjarak 2009). Overall, then, one sees a very strong correlation between capital inflow bonanzas, credit booms, and real estate bubbles.

Although the correlation between credit booms and real estate bubbles is robust, uncertainty surrounds the underlying causal mechanism. One mechanism that has received substantial attention is a shift in relative prices caused by real exchange rate appreciation. Reinhart and Reinhart (2009: 39) explain the logic as follows: "the pressures for the exchange rate to appreciate stem both from an increased demand for the local assets (which may or may not lead to an asset price boom or bubble) as well as from an increase in aggregate demand for both traded and non-traded goods. As long as the supply of the non-traded good is not perfectly elastic, the relative price of non-traded goods increase (i.e., a real exchange rate appreciation)" (see also, Calvo, Leiderman, and Reinhart 1993). The initial rise in real estate prices induced by the real exchange rate appreciation thus increases the supply of credit available for real estate investment, and this increased supply of credit to real estate further increases demand in that sector, pushing prices up still further (Herring and Wachter 2003). The secondary increase in real estate prices attracts additional investment, and so the cycle gathers momentum as it feeds back on itself. As the credit boom evolves, therefore, the banking system allocates an increasing share of credit to real estate and associated activities. In somewhat broader terms, investment shifts away from the less internationally competitive traded goods and toward activities in the sheltered sector where returns are rising (Terrones 2004: 154; Tornell and Westermann 2002).

In the third and final stage of the cycle, systemic banking crises occur. This trigger for banking crises differs substantially from conventional wisdom. Conventional wisdom holds that banking crises occur as a consequence of problems on the liability side of the balance sheet. In the standard bank run model, panics trigger bank runs that exhaust the bank's liquidity. Runs on individual banks have system-wide consequences as a result of interbank relationships. Thus, failure in one bank can ripple through the system and bring other banks down too. Most postwar systemic banking crises do not conform to this bank run model. Instead, postwar systemic banking crises have originated on the asset side of the balance sheet. In particular, problems have arisen when assets lose value rapidly as bubbles deflate. Such dynamics characterized the Nordic banking crises of the late 1980s, the Japanese crisis in the 1990s, as well as the crises in European banking systems in 2008 (Ireland, Iceland, Belgium, so forth). None of these episodes gave rise to widespread bank runs; instead in all instances banks experienced large-scale problems caused by their exposure to real estate loans collateralized by homes whose values were falling sharply (Claessens et al. 2013: 20).

In summary, systemic banking crises since the early 1970s, in the Organisation for Economic Co-operation and Development (OECD) and emerging markets alike, have developed out of, and dramatically amplified large and persistent macroeconomic imbalances. In the first stage, a configuration of macroeconomic conditions generates a credit boom. In particular, a credit boom emerges from the positive feedback between sustained economic growth, pro-cyclical fiscal policy, and capital flow bonanzas. In the second stage, credit booms combine with overvalued currencies to spark asset price bubbles in the real estate sector. Over the course of the boom, the banking system allocates an increasing share of credit to real estate, and bank balance sheets thus become ever more exposed to developments within property markets. In the third stage, banking crises result when real estate bubbles deflate. Falling asset prices weaken bank balance sheets generally, push many banks into insolvency, and thus give rise to a systemic banking crisis.

Postwar Credit Booms, Bubbles, and Banking Crises

America's postwar experience conforms quite closely to this more general pattern. America's macroeconomic imbalances, characterized by the configuration of robust economic growth, pro-cyclical fiscal policy imparted by military buildups, and capital flow bonanzas have generated credit booms. Each credit boom generated an asset bubble; two centered on real estate and a third in equity markets. In the two real estate bubbles, asset price deflation precipitated a systemic banking crisis. Moreover, we see no credit booms, or real estate bubbles, or banking crises in the absence of a military buildup induced expansion. We look first at the correlation between pro-cyclical fiscal policy, growth, and capital flow bonanzas on the one hand and postwar credit booms on the other. Attention then turns to the impact of credit booms on asset prices, bank balance sheets, and banking system crises.

Macroeconomic Imbalances and Postwar Credit Booms

Like credit booms elsewhere in the world, America's postwar credit booms have emerged in the context of robust growth, pro-cyclical fiscal policy, and capital flow bonanzas. We have seen in previous chapters that postwar military buildups have imparted a persistent pro-cyclical stimulus that transformed what would likely have been typical expansions into extended economic booms. Indeed, we found that three of four postwar booms have been sustained by pro-cyclical stimulus provided by military buildups and that a deficit-financed military buildup never failed to stimulate a boom. Thus, we know already that two of the three factors that have combined to trigger credit booms elsewhere in the global economy have been jointly present in the American economy during the 1960s, 1980s, and 2000s.

The only variable lacking for the American experience is the frequency of capital flow bonanzas. The most common operational definition of a capital flow bonanza is a period in which capital inflows rise into the 20th percentile of recent country-specific history (Reinhart and Reinhart 2009). Applied to America's postwar experience, this threshold identifies two capital flow bonanzas: one that began in 1984 and ended in 1988; a second that began in 1998 and ended in 2006. In each bonanza, capital inflows increased by more than 100 percent. Capital inflows rose from almost 2 percent to almost 4 percent of GDP after 1983 and from 3 percent to almost 6 percent between 1998 and 2006. The Vietnam War boom did not generate a capital flow bonanza. This is not particularly surprising, given the tight restrictions most governments applied to cross-border capital flows in this period.

We can thus formulate expectations about when we are more and less likely to observe credit booms in the American economy. We are most likely to observe credit booms during the mid-1980s and mid-2000s. Both periods were characterized by configuration of all three factors: pro-cyclical fiscal stimulus, robust growth, and a capital flow bonanza. We are less likely to observe a credit boom in the economic booms of the 1960s and 1990s. Both periods exhibit two of the three relevant factors: the late 1960s were characterized by robust growth and a pro-cyclical fiscal policy, but lacked the capital flow bonanza; the late 1990s combined sustained economic expansion and a large capital flow bonanza, but lacked pro-cyclical fiscal stimulus. Finally, we are unlikely to observe a credit boom in any other period of America's postwar history: there are no other extended expansions nor did the United States experience other capital flow bonanzas. We thus expect credit booms only in the mid-1980s and mid-2000s.

To evaluate these expectations, I identified postwar credit booms and plotted them against these configurations. To identify credit booms, I employed the threshold approach that has emerged as the dominant methodology (Gourinchas, Valdes, and Landerretche 2001; Mendoza and Terrones 2008). This method identifies credit booms as periods in which credit rises substantially above normal levels. Normal level is defined in terms of historical variation, with the threshold typically set at 1.75 times the standard deviation of the detrended credit cycle. To identify American credit cycles, therefore, I detrended real credit per capita using a Hodrick Prescott filter. Because the data are quarterly I followed the standard approach and set the smoothing parameter to 1600. I then calculated the standard deviation of the detrended series, using time-varying standard deviations generated across a rolling window. I used a constant base year and quarter and expanded the window over time. I then calculated the threshold for a credit boom as 1.75 times the standard deviation (Mendoza and Terrones 2008).

The results suggest quite clearly that credit booms are highly likely given the configuration of pro-cyclical fiscal policy, economic expansions, and capital flow bonanzas and less likely in the absence of this configuration. Figure 6.1 plots the cyclical component of real credit per capita between 1955 and 2008. The two shaded areas of the figure enclose the time periods characterized by the configuration of pro-cyclical stimulus, ongoing expansion, and capital flow bonanza. Two of three postwar credit booms fall inside these time periods. The largest occurred in the mid-2000s, with credit rising sharply above the threshold in 2006 and 2007. The second largest postwar credit boom occurred in the mid-1980s, with credit again rising sharply above the full sample threshold value beginning in 1985 and persisting until the end of 1986. Thus, the economic expansions and capital flow bonanzas resulting from the two military buildups that have

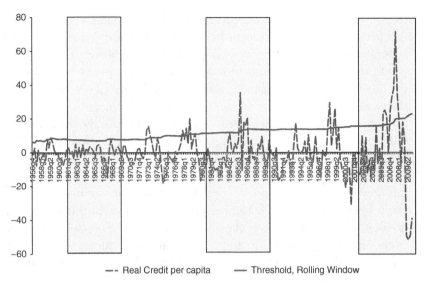

FIGURE 6.1. Postwar Credit Booms.

occurred since 1973 gave rise to large credit booms. And consistent with our expectations, the credit boom emerges in both instances in the middle rather than at the beginning of the expansions.

Credit booms rarely occur in the absence of this particular configuration of macroeconomic conditions. The economic expansion fuelled by the budget deficit resulting from the Vietnam War buildup did not generate a credit boom. Credit did expand sharply in 1967, peaking in the fourth quarter of 1967, but it fell just as sharply in the second quarter of 1968. Our framework suggests that the absence of a credit boom in this episode probably reflects the absence of a capital flow bonanza, which itself probably reflects the underdeveloped state of global capital mobility at the time. Nor does a credit boom emerge during any of the "normal" postwar expansions. Credit spiked twice during the 1970s, but in neither instance did it breach the threshold. Thus, the configuration of economic expansion, capital flow bonanza, and pro-cyclical fiscal policy correctly classifies the vast majority of America's postwar economic expansions.

Only one expansion is incorrectly classified. The economic boom of the 1990s exhibits two of the three factors typically associated with credit booms. This expansion was the longest of America's postwar booms and was accompanied by a large capital flow bonanza. Indeed, until the 2000s, the capital inflows registered in the last two years of the twentieth century were the largest of the postwar era. The episode fails to exhibit the third condition: pro-cyclical fiscal stimulus. Indeed, during this period the U.S. government budget steadily improved and recorded a surplus at the turn of the century. In this instance, however, a perceived productivity shock substituted for pro-cyclical fiscal policy by providing the initial burst of activity that generated widely shared optimism about the economic environment. However, one must also note that this is the smallest of the three postwar credit booms. Credit rose above the threshold in two quarters but averaged just slightly above the standard deviation for the seven quarters surrounding these peaks.

We observe a strong correlation between economic expansion, capital flow bonanzas, and pro-cyclical fiscal policy on the one hand and credit booms on the other. The presence and absence of this macroeconomic environment correctly classifies ten of eleven of postwar economic expansions into credit boom and non–credit boom categories. When all three are present, credit booms emerge and credit booms rarely emerge when one or more of these conditions are absent.

Credit Booms and Asset Price Bubbles

Each of America's three postwar credit booms generated an asset price bubble. The credit boom of the late 1990s generated an equity market bubble. Centered predominantly in the high-tech sector, this stock market bubble was driven by investor perceptions of the large productivity gains generated by the Internet revolution. The technology-heavy NASDAQ index rose from 1,000 to just above 5,000 between early 1997 and March of 2000. Enthusiasm for the tech sector pulled other indices up as well; the S&P 500 rose by 94 percent in the same period. Capital inflows fueled this bubble, with foreigners responsible for as much as half of total equity purchases in this period.

In contrast, the credit booms of the 1980s and 2000 generated real estate bubbles. Between 1983 and 1989, residential real estate values rose nationally by 20 percent. Real estate bubbles in this period were regional rather than national phenomena, however. In the Northeast, for instance, residential real estate appreciated by 15.5 percent per year between 1983 and 1987. In Boston, home prices rose by 115 percent between 1983 and 1987 (Case 1991, 1994; Federal Deposit Insurance Corporation 1997). In the New York metropolitan area, housing prices nearly tripled between 1981 and 1988 (Case 1994; Federal Deposit Insurance Corporation 1997). The appreciation was less steep in the West, where it averaged between 6.5 and 7.5 percent per year (Federal Deposit Insurance Corporation 1997). Home price appreciation of the mid-1980s pales in comparison to the magnitude and breadth of the appreciation that occurred in the 2000s. According to the Case-Shiller real home price index, housing values rose by 60 percent nationally between 2000 and 2006. Certain regions experienced even larger gains. Home prices more than doubled in Phoenix, Los Angeles, and Las Vegas between late 2001 and the middle of 2006.

And although each credit boom generated an asset bubble, no asset bubble emerged in the absence of a credit boom. We see no real estate bubbles in any other period of postwar history. According to the Case-Shiller real home price index, real estate values declined steadily between 1955 and 1970. And when real home prices rose during the second half of the 1970s, these gains were fully reversed by 1981. Nor did equity market bubbles arise outside of these eras. In the S&P 500 index, we see no persistent tendency toward atypically large year-to-year gains, which I define as three and a half times the average annual increase, outside of the three credit booms. In addition to the tech boom of the late 1990s, equity prices rose sharply between 1985 and late 1987, and again between 2003 and 2006. Thus, neither real estate nor equity market bubbles have emerged in the absence of a credit boom in America's postwar history.

America's postwar real estate bubbles emerged in a context of changing relative prices caused by an overvalued dollar. We have seen that the dollar appreciated sharply in the early 1980s and again in the late 1990s. In both instances, this relative price change caused private investment to shift into the non-traded sector. During the 1980s, residential real estate investment as a share of total investment rose from 20 percent in 1981 to 30 percent of total investment in 1986, 1987, and 1988. The real estate investment boom drove a sharp increase in new housing starts, which rose from 131,000 in 1983 to an average of 225,000 in 1986 and 1987 (Federal Deposit Insurance Corporation 1997: 340). The shift of investment into real estate was even more pronounced after 2001. Residential real estate investment rose from 25 percent of total private investment in 1997 to 37 percent of the total in 2005. Housing starts climbed from an average of 1.5 million per year during the 1990s to 2.3 million at the peak in early 2006 (U.S. Department of Commerce Census Bureau 2010). In both booms, therefore, investors responded to an over-valued dollar by shifting their attention to residential and commercial real estate.

Time series models indicate that the correlation between relative prices and investment in real estate is systematic and robust. I regressed five measures of year-to-year changes in sector-specific economic activity – manufacturing jobs, construction jobs, service jobs, finance jobs, and

TABLE 6.1. *The Real Exchange Rate and Activity in Manufacturing and Real Estate*

	Change in Manufacturing Jobs	Change in Service Jobs	Change in Finance Jobs	Change in Construction Jobs	Change in Residential Investment
Real Exchange Rate $_{t-1}$	−0.0001*** (0.00004)	0.0001** (0.00003)	0.00004*** (0.00001)	0.00002 (0.00002)	0.001*** (0.0004)
Real GDP Growth $_{t-1}$	0.11*** (0.02)	−0.04** (0.01)	−0.014** (0.01)	0.06*** (0.01)	−0.32** (0.18)
Change in Imports	−2.14e−11 (2.34e−09)				
Observations	34	34	34	34	34
Durbin–Watson	1.94		1.94	2.06	1.95
R^2	0.50	0.49	0.31	0.49	0.27
F Statistic	9.52 (0.0001)	11.68 (0.0001)	6.31 (0.02)	11.52 (0.0001)	5.05 (0.01)

real estate investment – against lagged values of the real exchange rate, real GDP growth, and a year counter to control for any possible time trend. I employed the level of the real exchange rate because my primary hypothesis is that resources shift out of manufacturing activities and into real estate when the currency is overvalued rather than in response to a positive change in the exchange rate. The results of the analysis are presented in Table 6.1.

The models suggest that an over-valued dollar has economic activity to shift out of the traded goods sector and into real estate. On the one hand, we see substantial evidence that the dollar's real exchange rate affects employment in manufacturing and services. The negative and significant coefficient in model one indicates that in periods of a strong dollar manufacturing's share of total employment falls. The positive coefficient on the real exchange rate in model two indicates that in periods of a strong dollar, the service sector's share of employment rises. The magnitude of the relationship is substantial. A one standard deviation appreciation of the dollar reduces manufacturing's share of total employment and increases the service sector's share by 1 percent of the total workforce. During the two buildup-induced booms, the dollar appreciated by roughly 30 percent, or three standard deviations, thereby shifting as much as 3 percent of the total labor force, between three and four million workers, from manufacturing into services. We see similarly that a strong dollar increases the number of jobs in the financial sector. In addition, the analysis reveals a positive and significant relationship between the dollar and residential real estate investment's share of total fixed investment. The magnitude of the estimated effect is plausible; a 10 percent dollar appreciation is associated with a one-point increase in residential real estate's share of total investment. Finally, we fail to identify a significant direct relationship between the real exchange rate and construction jobs.

Overall, then, we find substantial evidence to support the proposition that during the 1980s and again in the 2000s, an over-valued dollar encouraged structural change of the American economy. As the dollar strengthened, jobs and investment in manufacturing declined. Rather than remaining idle, however, labor and capital that are shed by manufacturing are redeployed in service sector activities and, a significant share is drawn into real estate activity. The number of housing starts increases, the amount of investment in residential investment increases, and the number of people employed in construction and finance expand. The number of people directly affected is significant. During the 1980s, the manufacturing sector shed about two million jobs while construction and finance gained slightly more than two million jobs. During the 2000s, the manufacturing sector shed three and a half million jobs while construction and finance added just under two million jobs.

Asset Price Deflation and Banking Crises

America's postwar real estate bubbles have produced systemic banking crises. They have done so because over the course of the boom the banking system becomes increasingly exposed to developments in real estate markets. During the 1980s, residential and commercial property mortgages became an increasingly important share of the assets held by thrifts and commercial banks' total assets (Boyd and Gertler 1994). Nationally, the ratio of real estate lending to total assets rose from 18 to 27 percent between 1980 and 1990 – a 50 percent increase. In the Northeast, where the bubble was most pronounced, real estate lending increased from 25 percent of total bank assets to 51 percent of total assets in the same period (Federal Deposit Insurance Corporation 1997: 151). The same trend is evident during the 2000s. Outstanding mortgage debt more than doubled over the boom, peaking at $14.5 trillion in 2007 (Federal Reserve System 2007). Of this, a little more than half ($7.5 trillion) was held in the form of mortgage-backed securities and collateralized debt

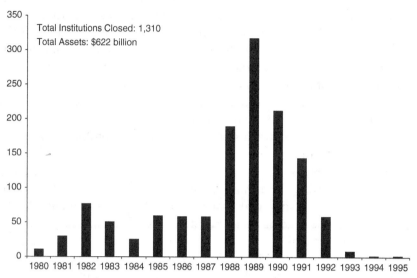

FIGURE 6.2. Failed Savings and Loan Associations.

obligations. Government agencies held about $4 trillion of this, and private institutions, especially special purpose vehicles (SPVs) held the balance. Over time, SPV balance sheets became increasingly concentrated on mortgages. In 2001, mortgages accounted for just less than half of the yearly net increase of SPV financial assets; by 2005 mortgages accounted for 99 percent of the net increase of SPV financial assets (Board of Governors of the Federal Reserve System 2012). As a result, by 2007 mortgages constituted 67 percent of total SPV financial assets – up from 40 percent in 2001.

As housing prices fell as the bubble deflated the balance sheets of financial institutions deteriorated sharply. Thrifts and commercial banks failed in record numbers between 1988 and 1992. The savings and loan industry had been struggling since the late 1970s, but failures in the early 1980s didn't approach the number of insolvencies after 1988 (Figure 6.2). Indeed, approximately half of all savings and loans institutions, with combined assets totaling $568 billion, failed between 1984 and 1997, with the largest number of failures occurring between 1988 and 1993. Commercial banks also failed in record numbers; 1,394 FDIC insured commercial banks with combined assets totaling $214 billion (about 7.5 percent of total commercial bank assets) failed or needed assistance between 1984 and 1992 (Figure 6.3).

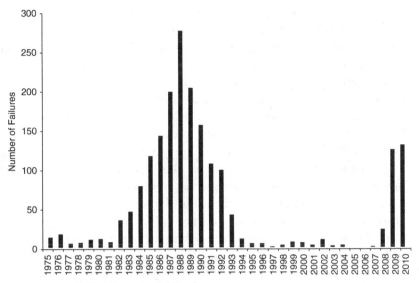

FIGURE 6.3. Failed Commercial Banks.

A wider variety of financial institutions failed in 2008–2010 as a consequence of differences in mortgage financing. Fewer commercial banks – only 181 by the end of 2010 – failed after 2008 than in the late 1980s. On average, however, each failed bank was substantially larger than its counterpart in the 1980s; consequently, the commercial banks that did fail accounted for 16 percent of all commercial bank assets – more than twice the share of the late 1980s. In addition, many non-bank mortgage lenders failed, such as American Home Mortgage, Countrywide (purchased by Bank of America), and NovaStar (no longer in mortgage lending). The five largest investment banks in the United States either failed or were merged as a consequence of their direct or indirect exposure to mortgage-backed securities. Finally, the two major government sponsored entities, Fannie Mae and Freddie Mac, were placed in conservatorship and recapitalized by the U.S. government. Thus, highly correlated overexposure to a collapsing real estate bubble triggered systemic banking crises in the United States.

No systemic banking crisis occurred outside of these two episodes. On average, five FDIC-insured banks failed each year between 1950 and 1980. In only two years did the number of bank failures exceed twice the standard deviation: thirteen banks failed in 1975 and seventeen banks failed in 1976. Combined, the assets of these failed banks amounted to only one-quarter of 1 percent of total commercial bank assets. And although one large and systemically important bank (Continental Illinois) failed in the early 1980s as a consequence of its indirect exposure to the Texas oil boom, financial regulators managed to prevent this failure from sparking a wider crisis (Federal Deposit Insurance Corporation 1997). Nor did the collective default of Latin American debtors in the early 1980s spark a systemic banking crisis. As one FDIC study summarized: "no large U.S. banks failed [during the 1980s] because of delinquent or nonperforming LDC loans" (Federal Deposit Insurance Corporation 1997: 208).

America's postwar banking history thus conforms to the empirical model that has generated banking crises in other countries since 1973. Large and persistent macroeconomic imbalances characterized by robust growth, capital flow bonanzas, and pro-cyclical fiscal policy generated credit booms. Credit booms generated asset price bubbles centered on real estate. The sustained shift in the share of investment allocated to real estate substantially increased the banking system's correlated exposure to developments in the real estate sector. Once the bubble popped, bank balance sheets deteriorated as the value of a substantial share of their assets fell sharply.

The Vietnam War Boom and the Dollar Crisis

The Vietnam War boom would appear to be an exception to the pattern we see in the 1980s and 2000s. For in contrast to the buildups sparked by the Soviet invasion of Afghanistan and the War on Terror, the Vietnam War buildup did not spark a credit boom, an asset bubble, or a banking crisis. The Vietnam War boom isn't an exception, however, for it did generate financial instability, but this instability manifested in a different form. Rather than generate an asset bubble and a systemic banking crisis, the Vietnam War boom generated a currency crisis in which markets attacked the dollar in anticipation of an inevitable devaluation.

First generation models of balance of payments crises help us understand why the Vietnam War boom generated a dollar crisis (Flood and Garber 1984; Krugman 1979). These models argue that currency crises emerge from market reactions to government policies that are inconsistent with a pegged exchange rate. In general, an inconsistent policy is one in which the central bank finances a fiscal deficit. This policy mix is inconsistent with an exchange rate peg because of its impact on the government's foreign exchange reserves. The logic is the following. An expansionary policy mix reduces net exports, and this external deficit is paid for with foreign exchange reserves. These transactions occur in the foreign exchange market as the monetary authority supports the peg by selling reserves and buying its currency. Government reserves are finite, however, and when they run out the government must either tighten macroeconomic policy to remove the inconsistency or allow the currency to depreciate.

Market participants remain willing to hold the currency only if they believe the government will remove the inconsistency before exhausting its reserves. If they believe the government will not remove the inconsistency, they will dump the currency. And once markets begin to lose confidence, currency sales accelerate the rate at which the government depletes its foreign exchange reserves, thereby making it more likely that the government will run out of reserves and increasing the incentive for markets to dump the currency.

This model of currency crisis thus suggests that the expansionary policy mix produced by Johnson's Vietnam War escalation widened the U.S. balance of payments deficit. Currency markets responded to the deteriorating U.S. external balance by selling the dollar whenever new information indicated that the United States would not alter fiscal and monetary policy. Indeed, this is precisely the dynamic that unfolded between 1965 and 1968.

The U.S. balance of payments position deteriorated fairly sharply between 1965 and 1968, with the deficit more than doubling from $1.5 billion to $3.5 billion. Developments in the current and capital accounts drove this evolution. The current account surplus that the United States had run throughout the postwar era (and indeed since World War I) narrowed steadily after 1965. In part this reflected rising imports in response to buoyant domestic demand and in part this reflected increased government military expenditures abroad. The capital account improved by less than the deterioration of the current account. Net long-term investment remained negative, as American firms invested in recently liberalized and increasingly integrated Europe. The United States offset net long-term capital outflows by attracting short-term capital inflows from private and public agents in Europe and Japan. The United States financed the remaining deficit with its gold reserves. Rather than settle by shipping gold or by transferring gold from U.S. official reserves to foreign countries' official reserves, the United States preferred to issue claims to its gold reserves in the form of U.S. dollars pegged to gold at $35 an ounce.

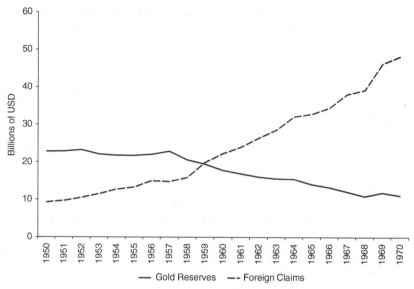

FIGURE 6.4. U.S. Foreign Liabilities and Gold Reserves.

The impact that these widening balance of payments deficits had on the relationship between U.S. gold reserves and foreign claims on this gold is clearly evident in Figure 6.4. The stock of foreign liabilities constitutes accumulated foreign claims on America's official gold reserves. The private sector held some of these claims and central banks held the rest. The stock of monetary gold constitutes the ability of the United States to satisfy these claims at the existing exchange rate. As Figure 6.4 illustrates, the gap between accumulated claims and available gold reserves grew larger as the 1960s progressed. By 1967, the United States held $12 billion of official gold reserves against $38 billion of accumulated foreign claims. Moreover, almost the entire official gold reserve was legally required as backing for the domestic currency and thus unavailable to settle foreign claims. Thus, the Johnson administration's expansionary policy mix was inconsistent with America's commitment to peg the dollar to gold at $35 an ounce.

The dollar's continued peg to gold thus came to depend on willingness of foreigners to continue to accumulate and hold dollars in spite of the obvious inconsistency between U.S. macroeconomic policy and the exchange rate peg. And as we saw in Chapter 5, much of U.S. domestic economic policy and international diplomacy in 1966 and 1967 revolved around encouraging foreigners to hold on to dollars. U.S. officials pressured foreign governments to refrain from exchanging their accumulated dollars for gold. American policymakers sought to defend the British pound's peg to keep the dollar out of the firing line. And American policymakers promised to alter macroeconomic policy to remove or at least lessen the inconsistency.

Such measures failed to prevent a massive speculative attack in early 1968. The timing of the attack is well explained by reference to unexpected developments in Vietnam and Congress that in combination suggested the inconsistent policies would persist and perhaps even worsen. First, the Tet offensive of January and February 1968 signaled that an American victory in Vietnam remained far in the future. Second, leaks revealed that the Chairman of the Joint Chiefs of Staff had requested on February 28 that the administration mobilize as many as 205,000 additional troops. This signaled that the cost of Vietnam would increase substantially – by as much as 40 percent in terms of its budgetary impact (Beecher 1968; Collins 1996; *New York Times* 1968b). Finally, these war-related news items came in the context of the refusal by the House Ways and Means Committee to pass the tax on tourism that Johnson had requested in his package of balance of payments measures that he announced on New Year's Day. This indicated that Congress was unlikely to enact the more important 10 percent war surtax that Johnson also requested. In combination, these events created the belief that the inconsistency between macroeconomic policy and the dollar's peg to gold would worsen rather than improve in the near term (Eichengreen 2000: 27). The administration's post-crisis investigation into the crisis concluded that these leaks about unexpected difficulties in Vietnam played a key role in triggering the market's attack against the dollar. Newly appointed Secretary of Defense Clark Clifford's investigation of the leaks led to a broad perception in "high Administration circles" that they "contribut[ed] to the recent gold crisis" – a crisis that was characterized at the time as the most severe episode of financial instability since the early 1930s (*New York Times* 1968a).

The Vietnam War boom thus generated financial instability of a different kind through the identical set of macroeconomic imbalances. The expansionary macroeconomic policy mix resulting from the buildup was inconsistent with the dollar's exchange rate peg. As foreign claims against America's gold reserves rose, market participants launched a speculative attack in March of 1968 that threatened to deplete America's gold reserves. U.S. efforts to sustain the system by refusing to sell monetary gold in the private market and by pressuring surplus governments to hold dollars merely delayed the system's inevitable collapse. Hence, when the run on the dollar resumed in 1970, American policymakers abandoned the remaining official commitment to gold convertibility.

Conclusion

Every postwar boom has generated a crisis. The specific nature of each crisis – whether they manifested as a currency or a banking crisis – varied as a function of institutional arrangements. At the broadest level, exchange rate arrangements determined whether an imbalance generated a currency or a banking crisis. The pegged exchange rate regime of the Bretton Woods system transformed imbalances into dollar overhang and a currency crisis. Under Bretton Woods' rules, the Federal Reserve was required to maintain the dollar's peg to gold. After 1965, maintaining this peg required the Fed to expand the money supply as the Vietnam War buildup produced budget deficits. However, by accommodating fiscal policy, the money supply expanded, the balance of payments deficit widened, and foreign central banks and market participants accumulated dollars. As the boom progressed, foreign claims rose relative to gold reserves, and the growing dollar overhang created the widespread expectation that the U.S. government would eventually devalue the dollar against gold. These beliefs generated speculative attacks whenever participants feared that devaluation was imminent.

With a floating currency, persistent macroeconomic imbalances have generated banking crises. Because the Federal Reserve has not been obligated to defend a particular peg the dollar, budget deficits have pushed interest rates up, attracted foreign capital, and strengthened the dollar. Investment shifted into the non-traded sector and the banking system steadily accumulated claims against real estate. Over time, and as a consequence, banking system stability became progressively more concentrated on developments in real estate markets. As market participants realized that real estate was overvalued and the mortgages they collateralized would soon trade at a steep discount from face value the bubble popped and the price correction weakened bank balance sheets.

The structural and regulatory environment influenced how banking crises unfolded as well as its global magnitude. The savings and loan crisis emerged in the context of a restrictive regulatory environment. This regulatory environment separated commercial and investment banking, thereby preventing commercial banks from underwriting and trading in securities, and tightly restricted branch and interstate banking. This regulatory environment yielded a traditional mortgage financing system in which thrifts extended long-term mortgages that they held on their balance sheets financed largely by federally insured deposits from a large number of small savers. Within this structure, foreign exposure to the impact of the deflating real estate bubble on the balance sheets of the thrifts was quite limited. As the real estate bubble popped, bank balance sheets deteriorated sharply, but in the context of the traditional model there was limited counterparty exposure. Moreover, because deposits were insured, there were few bank runs. Indeed, the crisis was more a chronic bleeding than a rapid collapse. As Robert Litan, a Brookings Institution specialist in banking and finance, observed at the time, "we have had headline after headline on the thrift crisis, but no erosion of confidence" (Nash 1988). The S&L crisis had limited global magnitude because few foreign investors held U.S. mortgages as assets, and few foreigners had entrusted significant deposits to or made large capital investments in thrifts. Japanese institutions, for instance, invested heavily in the U.S. during the decade, but preferred securities and direct investment to bank assets (Hung, Pigott, and Rodrigues 1989; Kawai 1995).

The subprime crisis developed within a different regulatory environment. The Riegle–Neal Act of 1994 removed barriers to interstate and branch banking. Perhaps ironically, this reform reflected in part the belief that geographic diversification would allow banks to avoid the regional concentration of mortgage exposures believed to have been responsible for the savings and loan crisis. The subsequent Financial Modernization Act of 1999 removed the last vestiges of the Glass–Steagall wall separating commercial from investment banking. These regulatory changes, along with financial innovation, accelerated the transformation of mortgage financing from a geographically limited and bank-based and deposit-based model to one based on debt finance, securitization, and geographic diversification. Because the large financial institutions borrowed to purchase and hold mortgage-backed securities, declining asset prices generated substantial counterparty risk. Problems that had their origins in mortgage finance thus spread rapidly through the financial system. And because only a small portion of these bank liabilities were federally insured, falling asset values led to a dramatic and sustained run on the shadow banking system. The crisis had a large global impact because American financial institutions funded their activities in part by borrowing abroad and sold the mortgage-backed securities they created to foreign institutions. As a result, foreign institutions became highly exposed to the developments in the American real estate market. Problems that originated in the United States thus spread quickly to foreign financial institutions.

Why didn't the imbalances of the 1980s and 2000s generate currency crises as well as banking crises? Such so-called twin crises have been quite common in the postwar era. Twenty-eight percent of banking crises since 1975 have been accompanied by currency crises (Laeven and Valencia; see also Kaminsky and Reinhart 1999). The absence of dollar crises in these episodes is all the more surprising given that so many very prominent observers feared that American imbalances during the 1980s and 2000s would produce dollar crises rather than banking crises. As Paul Krugman (2007b) noted, a broad consensus held that the U.S. current account deficit between 2002 and 2006 was unsustainable, and that adjustment would require dollar devaluation. The open question concerned whether adjustment would feature a soft or hard landing. Nouriel Roubini and Brad Setser predicted a hard landing, involving a large dollar depreciation, a sharp increase of interest rates, and a decline of U.S. and world growth (Roubini and Setser 2005a). Identical concerns prevailed during the mid-1980s (Krugman 1985; Marris 1985). Marris (1985: 240), for instance, predicted a hard landing: "What few seem to realize is that at some point in the near future, people's *ex ante* willingness to increase their exposure in dollars is going to fall to zero and, indeed, turn negative," generating an abrupt decline of the dollar.

American imbalances did not generate twin crises for two connected reasons. First, markets (and central banks) were not financing the U.S. "current account deficit" per se; they were purchasing a variety of dollar-denominated assets. Hence, the sustainability of the U.S. imbalance revolved around the value of the assets that investors purchased. This was quite different from the situation that prevailed during the late 1960s, when the official promise to convert dollars to gold at $35 an ounce provided a single focal point for investor decisions. Second, investors distinguished between different dollar-denominated assets even as the crisis broke. Here the U.S. experience differed sharply from that of other countries. When investors discovered widespread insolvencies in the Thai banking system in 1997 or the Icelandic banking system in 2008, for instance, they sold as many local currency denominated assets as they could. This economy-wide flight to safety exhausted foreign exchange reserves and thereby forced large devaluations. In contrast, market concern about the solvency of American investment banks and uncertainty about the value of mortgage-backed securities triggered a selloff and froze interbank lending. Yet, rather than dump all dollar denominated assets, investors bought U.S. government debt securities. As a result, the dollar strengthened and U.S. interest rates fell. The role of U.S. government debt as the benchmark global safe asset thus stabilized the dollar even in the midst of a system-wide crisis of American finance. The absence of a currency crisis was thus in large part a consequence of American structural power – the central role played by U.S. government debt and American bond markets in the contemporary global financial system.

Finally, although one might argue that the correlation between build-ups and bubbles that I highlight here is coincidental rather than causal, the fact that the American experience fits squarely within the more general pattern of banking and currency crises that have occurred elsewhere in the postwar era suggests otherwise. In this general pattern, capital inflow bonanzas spark a credit boom. The credit boom generates an asset bubble as new investment chases capital gains from rapid asset price appreciation. When asset prices deflate, financial institutions whose balance sheets are overly concentrated in the deflating assets are rendered insolvent. Currency crises have emerged whenever markets have perceived an inconsistency between a government's macroeconomic policy mix and its pledge to maintain a pegged exchange rate. America's postwar crises depart from these general patterns only in the specific sparks that ignite the bubbles and generate the policy inconsistencies. America's financial and monetary crises have been indirect consequences of the booms generated by America's deficit-financed military buildups.

7

The Political Economy of American Hegemony

> America's unipolar moment is over. It ... ended with the collapse of Lehman
> Brothers on September 15, 2008.
>
> Robert J. Art[1]

The Obama administration inherited a mess when it entered office in
January 2009. The country remained on a war footing, with more than
160,000 troops in Iraq and 38,000 more stationed in Afghanistan (Belasco
2009). The financial system remained weak, with memories of the collapse
of 2008 strong. The national economy had contracted at the annual rate
of 8.3 percent in the last quarter of 2008 and continued to shrink at an
annual rate of 5.4 percent in the first quarter of 2009. As economic activity
collapsed, the budget deficit swelled to almost 10 percent of gross domestic product (GDP). Consequently, much of the administration's energy and
attention have been directed at cleaning up this mess, at financial reform
and retrenchment – reducing America's overseas commitments.

Regulatory reform was enacted in 2010 via the Dodd–Frank Wall
Street Reform and Consumer Protection Act. Among other things, the
Dodd–Frank Act consolidated existing regulatory agencies and created
the Financial Stability Oversight Council and Office of Financial Research.
In addition, the Act established new regulations as well as a new resolution regime with responsibility to step in to liquidate insolvent institutions not covered by the FDIC. Global retrenchment has progressed more
slowly. The administration withdrew all U.S. forces from Iraq, and began

---

[1] Art (2012: 15).

withdrawing troops from Afghanistan in 2012. Moreover, adherence to the "don't do stupid sh*t" principle has led the Obama administration to resist pressure to accept new and potentially costly obligations, such as its non-intervention in the Syrian civil conflict. It is not unreasonable to suggest that the Obama presidency has been characterized by financial system reform and global retrenchment.

Obama is not the first to be forced to repair the damage imparted by the administration that preceded him. Indeed, retrenchment and reform have been the typical final stage of the political economic of imbalance. President George H. W. Bush inherited the S&L crisis and a large budget deficit from the Reagan administration and spent considerable energy – and most of his political capital with the Republican Party – bailing out the S&L industry, enacting new financial regulation to ensure that we would never again experience a real estate bubble, and raising taxes to help reduce the deficit. President Gerald R. Ford inherited the economic mess that LBJ had started and that Nixon had dramatically worsened. In each instance, administrations sought to restore financial stability and reduce America's overseas military obligations.

This final chapter, therefore, focuses on regulatory reform and retrenchment. After a brief summary of the argument I have developed, my focus becomes largely prescriptive: should the United States re-regulate and retrench? I argue that this study suggests that what the United States needs is a more responsible form of global engagement. I draw on the perspective I have developed in the preceding chapters to develop this recommendation in three steps. First, post-crisis reform expects far too much from financial regulation. Avoiding future asset bubbles requires a more responsible fiscal policy. Second, post-crisis retrenchment leans far too heavily on fear of the long-run consequences of deficits and debt. I argue that far greater costs arise from the global economic instability and loss of goodwill among our allies caused by deficit-financed buildups. Retrenchment is thus far less important than responsible global engagement. Finally, shifting to a strategy of responsible global engagement requires the American public to reengage with foreign policy, something most likely to be achieved through the establishment of universal national service.

Institutions, Financial Power, and the Political Economy of Imbalance

American hegemony has been characterized by a political economy of imbalance: a repeating pattern of buildup, boom, and bust. An unexpected national security threat sparks a military buildup. The United States pays for the additional military power by borrowing rather than by raising taxes or reducing spending in other programs. The resulting budget deficits impart large, persistent, pro-cyclical stimulus that transforms an ongoing expansion into a boom. Financial and monetary fragility develop over the course of the boom and accumulating system fragility eventually sparks a crisis. The pattern has occurred each time the United States has increased military spending sharply since 1960: the Vietnam escalation beginning in 1965, the Carter-Reagan buildup beginning in 1980, and the buildup for the wars in Afghanistan and Iraq following the attacks of 9/11. The only buildup that didn't have this impact, the Korean War, was the only buildup the government paid for by raising taxes.

This political economy of imbalance has been the consequence of how America's political institutions and its global financial power channel the government's response to national security shocks. The decentralized nature of America's political institutions creates a multiple veto player system that constrains policy to small movements around the status quo most of the time. Because large change requires consent from so many actors, and because actors' ideal points are heterogeneous, most changes in policy are quite small. Large changes in policy are thus rare, and in the case of defense spending have come in response to exogenous security shocks that cause veto players' ideal points to converge on a much larger (or smaller) defense budget. And though veto players agree on the need to increase spending sharply in the midst of the urgency of these security emergencies, they continue to hold divergent views as to how to pay for the additional military power. As a consequence, military buildups generate large budget deficits as veto players battle over whether to raise taxes or reduce welfare spending.

American financial power transforms these budget deficits into fiscal stimulus. One might imagine that rising borrowing by the government would crowd out borrowing for investment purposes in the private sector. Hence the budget deficit wouldn't add demand to the economy it would merely redistribute spending from the private sector to government. America's financial power, its ability to borrow from the rest of the world in large amounts for extended periods at low cost, eliminates this crowding out effect at home. As government borrowing rises, the upward pressure on U.S. interest rates attracts capital from abroad. In the contemporary global economy, therefore, increased government borrowing doesn't crowd out private investment or consumer credit. So instead of merely redistributing spending, America's budget deficits add to aggregate demand. And because deficit-financed military buildups have occurred in the midst of or persisted well into an ongoing expansion, their stimulus creates the booming economic environment within which financial fragility develops.

America's political economy of imbalance has had a tremendous impact on global political economy. It has generated large global current account imbalances as well as the cross border capital flows necessary to finance them. It has repeatedly generated widespread concern among global policymakers about global stability in the face of the adjustment that would one day have to occur. Would this adjustment come abruptly with a dollar crash, or could cooperation among the large powers produce a more gradual path? Negotiations about adjustment – what policies to use and which states would bear the costs – have generated substantial political conflict. The United States has pressured its trade partners to adjust by increasing consumption and revaluing their currencies while America's partners have pressured the U.S. government to get a handle on its fiscal problems. And a substantial amount of attention has focused on redesigning institutions and rebuilding confidence following the major crises these imbalances have spawned. Indeed, it is only a small overstatement to suggest that much of postwar global political economy has revolved around the effort to manage the consequences of America's buildup-induced imbalances.

I am sure that more than a few readers believe that my explanation of America's external deficits has placed too much emphasis on America's deficit-financed military buildups and paid too little attention to the contribution of policy in the surplus economies. After all, didn't the surplus states undervalue their currencies and suppress domestic consumption? I readily accept that policies in the surplus economies played an important role in generating current account surpluses. And yes, Asian and European surpluses had to be offset by deficits elsewhere in the system. But the fact that some economies somewhere in the system had to run deficits does not imply that the United States had to do so. The United States could have run a current account surplus too; it chose not to do so. And by choosing not to, the United States winds up imposing substantial costs on the rest of the world. It would be good if we could avoid repeating this pattern a fourth time. Avoiding repetition will require new thinking about how financial crises emerge and how deficit spending affects the economic foundations of American power.

The Limits of Financial Regulation

As a first step toward new thinking, this book encourages scholars, policymakers, and the media to embrace a broader conception of the genesis of the 2008 financial crisis, and of financial crises more generally, than one finds in most treatments. The typical approach to crises assumes that financial fragility and the consequent financial instability have entirely financial origins. They emerge from excessive risk taking by financiers who operate within the context of inadequate regulatory regimes. This core logic is then reinforced by considerations of the growing complexity of the financial system and the prevailing free market ideology. Such were the conclusions reached by the official Financial Crisis Inquiry Commission (Financial Crisis Inquiry Commission 2011). Such is the central premise of almost every book that has been written about the causes of the crisis until now (see, e.g., Blinder 2013; Johnson 2010; McCarty, Poole, and Rosenthal 2013).

My perspective suggests that this standard account of the crisis is incomplete and a solution based entirely on reforms of financial regulation is inadequate. There is no question that financial institutions invested too heavily in real estate and as a consequence the financial system froze when the real estate bubble popped. There is no question that regulators failed entirely to recognize the buildup of systemic risk as the housing bubble developed. Nor can one object to efforts to enhance regulatory capacity in an age of growing financial complexity. The argument developed in this book, however, suggests that such reform will be insufficient to prevent future crises. Much as the Financial Institutions Reform, Recovery, and Enforcement Act of 1989, enacted in response to the S&L crisis, failed to prevent the subprime crisis, so the Dodd–Frank Act will be unable to prevent the next real estate bubble.

My perspective, inspired in many ways by Hyman Minsky's financial instability hypothesis, suggests that understanding the development of financial crises requires us to recognize that financial institutions respond to signals from the wider political economy within which they are embedded (Minsky 1986). Minsky argued that finance entails a fundamental uncertainty: Will the future cash flow generated by a debt-financed real asset be sufficient to repay the debt with which it was purchased? And this uncertainty attaches not solely to the individual or corporate entity that contracted the debt, but also to the broader economic environment within which this transaction occurs. If a banker lends millions to GM to construct a new plant, will GM sell enough cars to service the loan? The answer has only partly to do with the inherent quality of GM cars and management. The future state of the macroeconomy is equally relevant. Will growth be sufficiently robust to keep unemployment down and the demand for cars high? Will interest rates be low enough to make buying the cars being produced possible? Will the dollar move in a direction that enhances the profitability of producing cars in the United States or in a direction that makes Japanese and Korean cars more attractive? What will happen to the price of oil over the next few years, and how will that affect the demand for the cars to be produced? And financial institutions develop expectations about these unknowns by collecting information from the wider economic environment.

Fiscal policy plays a central role in generating the information that shapes the financial system's expectations. American fiscal policy since 1960 has played this role in two ways. First, the large budget deficits, as well as the political institutions that constrain efforts to reduce these deficits, have provided a steady source of demand that has kept the economy humming along. And because it is so difficult to reduce budget deficits, the financial system can assume that demand will remain strong for an extended period. As Minsky argued, "The deficits of Big Government are the sufficient condition" for an investment boom and financial crisis. "By sustaining aggregate demand, they sustain corporate profits and feed secure assets into portfolios" (Minsky and Kaufman 2008: 106). Second, America's budget deficits have caused the dollar to appreciate as foreign capital has flowed into the United States. This relative price shift has encouraged investment funds to flow toward the non-traded sector, especially real estate. In the United States, the exchange rate has thus provided a powerful signal around which financial institutions have coordinated their behavior. The focus on fiscal policy thus provides an answer to the question of why "it" happened then.

Large fiscal shocks can occur in response to an array of noneconomic developments. In postwar America, the largest budget shocks have been triggered by natural disasters such as Hurricane Katrina, and by national security shocks. And because the timing of these budget shocks bears no relation to the economy's position in the business cycle, they are more likely to occur in the midst of an ongoing expansion than during a recession. The persistent pro-cyclical nature of the resulting fiscal impulse thus creates highly optimistic expectations about future profits. Of course, military buildups need not be the cause of fiscal shocks; it just happens to be the case that in postwar America they were. Recognizing the role that national security shocks have played in driving major fiscal policy shocks adds a second layer of explanation for the development of the financial crisis.

It is within this broader macroeconomic context that the financial system sometimes evolves steadily toward increasing fragility. The initial push into real estate is rewarded with rising housing prices, not least because the supply of new homes lags behind the sudden increase of demand. The large capital gains thus induce additional investment into real estate, and prices rise again. The system in turn creates the credit necessary to finance these desired purchases. And thus over time the financial system becomes increasingly exposed to real estate that becomes progressively more overvalued. Eventually it becomes apparent that the real assets will not generate the income necessary to liquidate the liabilities held against them. Optimism about the future evaporates, banks stop lending against the underlying asset, and asset prices deflate. And as financial firms are uncertain about which among them holds large quantities of mortgage-related debt, they cease lending to each other as well.

Can monetary policy or financial regulation prevent asset bubbles from developing given an underlying fiscal imbalance? Many have blamed monetary policy for the subprime crisis. John Taylor, for instance, has argued that the Federal Reserve kept interest rates too low for too long, thereby sparking the credit bubble that fuelled the asset bubble (Taylor 2007, 2009, 2010). The government's *Financial Crisis Inquiry Commission* (2011: 125) agreed, concluding that "the monetary policy of the Federal Reserve, along with capital flows from abroad, created conditions in which a housing bubble could develop." Yet, one wonders if we also expect too much from monetary policy. Minsky argued that the central bank does not control the money supply or the growth of credit. The banking system creates credit as a function of its expectations of future profits. Any effort by the central bank to constrain the banking system's creation of credit by manipulating reserve requirements merely encourages banks to innovate and expand their off-balance sheet activities. Moreover, in an open economy an attempt to raise interest rates will attract more foreign investment.

Nor can regulation prevent crises of this kind. Banking crises come in a variety of flavors. Regulation may be quite effective in limiting the frequency of plain vanilla crises, such as those that occur as cascading failures sparked by the collapse of a single institution. The 1984 failure of Continental Illinois, which was the country's seventh largest bank at the time, did not trigger a systemic crisis, and prudential regulation may have been the reason. But regulation may be the wrong instrument to prevent crises of more exotic flavors because the conditions within which these crises develop do not appear dangerous. For instance, even as late as 2007 there was no consensus that the United States was in the midst of a housing bubble (see, e.g., McCarthy and Peach 2004; Smith and Smith 2006). How then could one argue that the financial system was too heavily exposed to overvalued assets? Nor was there any indication that the financial system was about to implode. The FDIC, for example, noted in its forecast for 2007, "FDIC-insured institutions continue to ride a string of six consecutive years of record earnings. Bank capital levels remain at historic highs, while loan performance has slipped only slightly from record levels" (Federal Deposit Insurance Corporation 2006). The International Monetary Fund was similarly sanguine: "default risk in the financial and insurance sectors remains relatively low, and credit derivatives markets do not indicate any particular financial stability concerns" (International Monetary Fund 2006: 26). And these evaluations occurred after the goose had already been cooked – by late 2006 the explosion of mortgage lending was over and real estate prices were in decline. The first tremors that signaled the onset of the crisis came in August of 2007. To have been effective, therefore, regulatory intervention would have to have occurred in 2004 and 2005. Yet, at that point there was even less evidence of systemic fragility.

Rather than treat these types of financial crises as the result of excessive risk taking by bankers operating in largely autonomous financial markets, we must recognize that financial markets are connected to the real economy and powerfully influenced by government fiscal policy decisions. And in postwar America, large fiscal shocks have been caused by military buildups undertaken in response to unexpected threats to national security. Limiting the recurrence of such crises thus requires a more responsible fiscal policy.

Retrenchment, Deficits, and American Power

"America's unipolar moment is over." Robert J. Art writes, "It ... ended with the collapse of Lehman Brothers on September 15, 2008" (Art 2012: 15). The case for retrenchment rests on a widely shared belief that America's current fiscal situation constrains the resources available to support a strategy of "deep engagement." "For the past two decades, American foreign policy ... has quite simply over-reached" (Haass 2013: 6). The over-reach has caused the United States to spend too much on wars in Iraq and Afghanistan and too little on the domestic economic foundations of power. As one recent defense of deep engagement sum-marizes, advocates of retrenchment claim that "'deep engagement' has high and rising costs that dwarf its benefits. The United States' decline relative to potential rivals makes it ever harder to maintain its multi-tudinous commitments, while its allies can afford to defend themselves and should no longer be 'subsidized'" (Brooks, Ikenberry, and Wohlforth 2013: 8) Retrenchment strives to rebalance these priorities – scale back America's overseas obligations, reduce military spending, and focus on restoring critical domestic infrastructure.

Contemporary calls for retrenchment echo practically identical con-cerns raised twenty-five years ago during the final years of the Cold War. The terms of debate during the late 1980s were provided by the "Imperial Overstretch Hypothesis" (IOH), which had been developed in independent work by Robert Gilpin and Paul Kennedy. The IOH offered as a theoretical and historical model in which the decline of hegemonic power occurred as a consequence of excessive global ambition. Robert Gilpin argued that the burden of defending a growing sphere of influ-ence places ever increasing demands on the hegemon's national income (Gilpin 1981: 162). Eventually, the hegemon faces a domestic fiscal crisis that manifests as "an increasingly severe political conflict over the allo-cation of national income among protection, consumption, and invest-ment" (Gilpin 1981: 166–167). Gilpin claimed that societies would be unable to reduce consumption in order to increase investment and would be thus unable to sustain the productivity gains required to defend their global sphere of influence.

Gilpin's academic argument moved into the public sphere in the late 1980s. Paul Kennedy advanced a very similar set of ideas, though Kennedy's treatment was historical as opposed to Gilpin's more theoretic. And unlike Gilpin, Kennedy sought to influence the direction of policy by arguing that the United States had overreached. "Decision-makers in Washington must face the awkward and enduring fact that the total of the United States's global interests and obligations is nowadays far too large for the country to be able to defend them all simultaneously" (Kennedy 1987: 36).

Although the IOH lost favor in the 1990s in the midst of America's unipolar moment, the hypothesis has reemerged to define the terms of the contemporary debate about retrenchment (see, e.g., Haass 2013; Layne 2012; Mason 2009). Robert Pape argued that the Bush adminis-tration's determination to fight wars in Iraq and Afghanistan was yielding an unprecedented decline of American power (Pape 2009). Christopher

Layne has asserted that though the IOH had been wrong in the 1980s, "this time it's real" (Layne 2012). "It now is evident," Layne argued, "that both the 1980s declinists and the unipolar pessimists were right after all ... The Great Recession has underscored the reality of US decline, and only "denialists" can now bury their heads in the sand and maintain otherwise" (Layne 2012: 204). And like Kennedy and Gilpin, Layne attributes America's decline in large part to the fiscal imbalances and debt burdens accumulated over the last fifteen years.

This book's perspective suggests that the IOH rests on an incomplete and misleading conception of the economic consequences of deficit-financed military spending. The IOH conceptualizes the hegemon's resource constraint in a closed economy context. Global finance is particularly noticeable for its absence. Instead, theorists assert that the hegemon confronts a binding national resource constraint in every period. Consequently, any resources that the hegemon allocates to defense reduce the resources available for private investment and thus reduce productivity growth and future income. The government is thus assumed to face a strict guns versus butter tradeoff.

The incorporation of financial power into the IOH model relaxes the hegemon's short-run constraint substantially. When a hegemon can borrow easily from the rest of the world, it no longer faces a binding national resource constraint in every period. Indeed, because foreign investors are willing to purchase financial assets denominated in the hegemon's currency, increased military spending does not crowd out private investment in the hegemon's economy. In the short run, therefore, total expenditures by the hegemon are not limited to currently available national resources. Deficit-financed military buildups need not have a negative impact on the future level of national income by reducing investment.

Moreover, deficits may have no long run impact on future income at all. Whether government debt reduces future income depends on the relationship between the return on government debt (the interest rate on government bonds) and the rate of economic growth rate. As long as the return on government debt is below the growth rate, debt service imposes a decreasing burden on national income. This is more than a theoretical possibility. Ball, Elmendorf, and Mankiw (1998) found that the rate of economic growth has been higher than the return on government debt for most of American history since 1870, and especially so since 1946. America's experience following World War II, during which robust postwar growth reduced the burden of America's war debt, offers a compelling recent example. All of this suggests that the concern about the long-run economic consequences of deficit-financed military spending is overwrought.

This is not to suggest that buildup-related deficits have been costless for American power; rather it is to suggest that all of the costs generated by deficits are contemporaneous. They manifest in the form of systemic instability and declining political influence. Michael Mastanduno has noted that in the postwar era the United States has been a system maker and a privilege taker (Mastanduno 2009). "The United States has created, maintained, defended, and expanded a liberal economic order to serve national economic and security interests ... The United States has [also] taken advantage of its privileged position within that international order to serve its own particular ends. It has employed its preponderant power at the core of the world economy to placate domestic constituencies and preserve the autonomy of central decision makers over U.S. foreign, defense, and macroeconomic policy. Across the bipolar and unipolar eras, the United States has been simultaneously a system maker and a privilege taker" (Mastanduno 2009: 122). Mastanduno's concept of privilege taking nicely captures the way the United States has exploited its financial power to respond to unexpected military challenges to the liberal international order.

But as privilege taker the United States has been a system breaker. Indeed, it is no small irony that America's determination to defend the postwar liberal order by exploiting its financial power has in every instance wound up weakening substantially key components of this order. Vietnam undermined the Bretton Woods system of exchange rates. The subprime crisis punctured turn-of-the-century confidence in liberal capital markets and international financial interdependence, pushed the global economy into recession, and brought rising trade barriers. A worse outcome was avoided only because international institutions facilitated a cooperative response (Drezner 2014). Even the Carter–Reagan buildup, which failed to generate a global crisis, eroded the political foundations of the international trade system, generated widespread concern about a dollar crisis, and produced a sharp stock market crash (Black Monday). One hardly exaggerates to suggest that America's deficit-financed military buildups have generated the most significant challenges to the economic components of this order.

America's exploitation of its financial power has also been costly in terms of global goodwill. America's reliance on its financial power generates political acrimony as the United States attempts to push the costs of adjusting to reduce American imbalances onto its creditors. As we have seen, during the last fifty years, the United States has pressured and cajoled its allies, trading partners, and principal creditors to purchase American military equipment, to revalue their currencies, and to coordinate their macroeconomic policies. In short, the United States has sought to deflect the costs of adjustment onto its creditors. Not surprisingly, America's allies do not always welcome these efforts.

And though America's creditors have been willing to cooperate to manage the consequences of American imbalances, they have done so grudgingly and in large part only because they recognize that they have little choice. But each episode erodes their goodwill. And each episode generates renewed discussion about creating some alternative to the U.S. dollar in order to reduce America's financial power (see, e.g., Eichengreen 2011; Helleiner and Kirshner 2009; Otero-Iglesias and Steinberg 2012, 2013). Thus, America's imbalances erode the willingness of America's allies and creditors to share the costs of adjustment and increase their determination to find a substitute for the dollar.

Retrenchment fails to address the actual source of America's waning global influence. The underlying problem generated by America's global reach isn't that deficits and debt weaken America's economic foundations. The problem is that the political economy of imbalance erodes America's global political capital. The irresponsible way in which the United States exploits its financial power creates global economic challenges; forces the costs arising from these challenges onto other states; and thus erodes the willingness of America's allies, trade partners, and primary creditors to support American policy. Retrenchment risks amplifying this loss of goodwill by increasing the uncertainty of allies about America's willingness to make good on the commitments it has embraced. In many respects, retrenchment is a costly overreaction. The solution to concerns about America's global power lies not in retrenchment; it lies in a more responsible form of global engagement.

Reengaging the American Public

How do we achieve a more responsible form of global engagement? The easy answer, of course, is that American engagement must rely less on military power and more on other forms of power. And when the United States does use force it should raise taxes rather than exploit its financial power to pay for it. The hard part is explaining how to bring about such a transformation in American policy. One might hope that changes in the international system will reduce U.S. reliance on military power. If the so-called Long Peace persists, then the United States might face fewer challenges to which military force is a useful response (Goldstein 2011; Pinker 2012). Yet, I am skeptical that we can depend on the evolution of history to reduce U.S. reliance of force. For even in this era of the Long Peace, the United States has deployed troops overseas almost 150 times (Eikenberry 2013). And while most deployments have been short and small, the two most recent wars have stretched the military's capacity and lasted longer than any others in American history.

Any transformation must therefore occur through American politics. Yet, finding domestic solutions is tricky, for as we have seen, the political economy of imbalance is not the strategy of a unified rational actor that we can change through persuasion. Instead, imbalances have been unintended consequences of the opportunity structure established by America's decentralized political institutions and its global financial power. Responsible policy thus requires some way to break the gridlock induced by American institutions. This is challenging; gridlock has been studied by the best students of American politics (Binder 2003; Mann and Ornstein 2012). This research has yet to identify the Archimedean Point from which an outside observer could leverage institutional change to solve problems. Consequently, even the most prominent scholars conclude that policy reform requires extrainstitutional change. McCarty, Poole, and Rosenthal (2013: 270–271), for instance, assert that "the best hope ... given the stability of the political system, is to begin to build a new public philosophy for dealing with the challenges of our time."

What should a new public philosophy look like to generate a more responsible global engagement? I believe that the requisite public philosophy is one that emphasizes civic engagement in foreign policy. During the last forty years the American public has disengaged from meaningful and informed discussion about foreign policy challenges. Between 2001 and 2013, the U.S. government spent approximately six trillion dollars fighting two wars. Close to seven thousand American soldiers were killed in action, approximately 59,000 were wounded, and an unknown number of others returned home with posttraumatic stress (United States Department of Defense 2014). And yet, according to a recent Pew Research Center study, two-thirds of the American public report that these wars never come up in the conversations they have with family and friends; half say that these wars have made no difference in their lives (Pew Research Center 2011). And what we observe in regard to these specific wars seems to characterize the public attitude toward foreign policy more generally. In poll after poll, the American public rarely ranks foreign policy issues among the most important problems facing the nation.

Many have attributed the American public's disengagement from foreign policy and decisions about the use of force to the shift from a draft-based to an all-volunteer military. Julian Zelizer (2010: 235) asserts that "eliminating the draft ... weakened the most immediate connection that existed between the national security state and average citizens." Andrew Bacevich claims that the results have been "anything but democratic." "Current arrangements have allowed and even encouraged Americans to disengage from war at a time when war has become all but permanent. Rather than being shared by many, the burden of service and sacrifice is borne by a few, with the voices of those few unlikely to be heard in the corridors of power" (Bacevich 2013; see also Bailey 2009; Eikenberry 2013). To put this in perspective, the wars in Afghanistan and Iraq were the longest in American history, and yet were fought by the smallest share of the American public – about one half of 1 percent – of any of America's wars (Pew Research Center 2011: 8). In contrast, for instance, 9 percent of the population fought in World War II, and about 2 percent fought in the wars in Korea and Vietnam.

The public seems fully aware that the burden of war fighting has been highly concentrated on a small segment of American society. According to this same Pew Center study, 83 percent of the American public believed that military personnel have made significant sacrifices over the last thirteen years. And only 43 percent of the same respondents thought that the American public at large had sacrificed significantly. Moreover, 70 percent responded that they thought this distribution of the burden was fair (Pew Research Center 2011: 63). By concentrating war fighting on to a very small proportion of the American public, the all-volunteer force has enabled the American public to view war as something other people do and as a consequence, as something that has no particular relevance to their lives. Understandably, they invest little energy becoming informed about foreign policy to influence its direction.

America's financial power has also encouraged the public to disengage from foreign affairs. The Gates Commission, convened by President Nixon in 1970 to evaluate the impact of shifting to an all-volunteer military, discounted concerns expressed at the time that ending the draft would reduce public engagement in decisions concerning the use of force (United States Government 1970). The Commission argued that any major expansion of military force would require additional revenue. And "if tax increases are needed or military spending claims priority

over other public spending, a broad public debate [will take place]"
(ibid: 155). Indeed, Commission members believed that "recent history
suggests that increased taxes generate far more public discussion than
increased draft calls" (ibid: 155). Thus, they concluded, an all-volunteer
force would actually produce greater public participation in decisions
about military force (ibid). America's financial power has undermined
completely this expectation by enabling politicians to use military force
without needing to ask the public to pay for it or scale back expenditures
on other government programs.

The end of the draft and the enhancement of America's financial power
have thus weakened substantially the democratic participation in and
constraint on decisions about the use of military power. Because the typical citizen bears no direct human or economic cost from the government's
use of force, he or she has little incentive to monitor and try to limit the
government's reliance on military power. As a result, the United States
probably pursues military solutions to its foreign policy challenges more
often than it would if the public expected to bear some of the human and
economic costs arising from military action (Eikenberry 2013).

How do we foster the civic engagement needed to constrain the executive branch's use of force? The most likely solution is instituting universal national service. The Aspen Institute's Franklin Project, initiated
in mid-2012, offers one approach. Retired General Stanley McChrystal
initiated the Franklin Project as a means to address his concern that the
typical American had no real understanding of what service to the nation
entailed. He was concerned in particular about the emergence of a huge
experiential gap between the fraction of the population that serves in the
military and the rest of the American public. He proposed as a means to
reduce this gap that every American serve for one year in either a military
or civilian capacity (The Franklin Project 2013). The Franklin Project
claims, and not without reason, that the Greatest Generation was forged
through such national service obligations, and as a consequence "voted
more, entered public service in greater numbers, and enjoyed much lower
levels of political polarization" (ibid: 5). One might hope that a renewed
culture of service would have a similar impact on the next generation.

Universal national service is no panacea. Yet, it can contribute impor-
tantly to the reconstitution of citizen engagement necessary to dampen
the political economy of imbalance and create a more responsible form
of American engagement in global politics. There is no guarantee that
such measures will prevent future imbalances and financial crises.
Financial markets are complex adaptive systems that react to and amplify

developments elsewhere in the global political economy. And while America's postwar deficit-financed military buildups have constituted a very important source of such developments, they are certainly not the only source. I do not claim, therefore, to have found a magic bullet with which to end financial instability. I do believe, however, that relying less on military power and paying for the wars we do fight will make us less likely to shoot ourselves in the foot.

References

9–11 Commission. 2004. *The 9–11 Commission Report.*

Ahearn, Raymond J. 1986. Protectionist Legislation in 1985. Washington, DC: Congress Research Service.

Ahearn, Raymond J., and A. Reifman. 1986. U.S. Trade Policy: Congress Sends a Message. In *Current US Trade Policy: Analysis, Agenda, and Administration. Conference Report*, eds. R. E. Baldwin and J. D. Richardson, pp. 98–130. Cambridge, MA: National Bureau of Economic Research.

——— 1988. Trade Legislation in 1987: Congress Takes Charge. In *Issues in the Uruguay Round. Conference Report*, pp. 67–86. Cambridge, MA: National Bureau of Economic Research.

Aizenman, Joshua, and Reuven Glick. 2006. Military Expenditure, Threats, and Growth. *Journal of International Trade & Economic Development* 15 (2): 129–155.

Aizenman, Joshua, and Yothin Jinjarak. 2009. Current Account Patterns and National Real Estate Markets. *Journal of Urban Economics* 66: 75–89.

Aldrich, John H., Christopher Gelpi, Peter Feaver, Jason Reifler, and Kristin Thompson Sharp. 2006. Foreign Policy and the Electoral Connection. *Annual Review of Political Science* 9: 477–502.

Alesina, Alberto, Filipe R Campante, and Guido Tabellini. 2008. Why Is Fiscal Policy Often Procyclical? *Journal of the European Economic Association* 6 (5): 1006–1036.

Alesina, Alberto, and Allan Drazen. 1991. Why Are Stabilizations Delayed? *The American Economic Review* 81 (December): 1170–1188.

Andrews, David M. 2006. Monetary Power and Monetary Statecraft. In *International Monetary Power*, ed. David M. Andrews, pp. 7–28. Ithaca, NY: Cornell University Press.

Andrews, Edmund L. 2008. Greenspan Concedes Error on Regulation. *New York Times*, October 23, p. B1.

Aronoff, Yael S. 2006. In Like a Lamb, out Like a Lion: The Political Conversion of Jimmy Carter. *Political Science Quarterly* 121 (3): 425–449.

Art, Robert J. 2012. Selective Engagement in an Era of Austerity. In *America's Path: Grand Strategy for the Next Administration*, eds. Richard Fontaine and Kristin M. Lord, pp. 11–27. Washington, DC: Center for a New American Security.

Bacevich,AndrewJ.2013.OnceaDuty,MilitaryServiceRecastasaRight.*TheBoston Globe*, February 2, 2013. Retrieved from http://www.bostonglobe.com/opinion/2013/02/02/military-personal-preference-trumps-collective-obligation/WmLYdiGUNYGsw2YpCYC2PJ/story.html

Bagwell, Kyle, and Robert W. Staiger. 2003. Protection and the Business Cycle. *Advances in Economic Analysis & Policy* 3 (1): 1–45.

Bailey, Beth. 2009. *America's Army: Making the All-Volunteer Force*. Cambridge, MA.: The Belknap Press of Harvard University Press.

Ball, Laurence, Douglas W Elmendorf, and N Gregory Mankiw. 1998. The Deficit Gamble. *Journal of Money, Credit and Banking* 39 (4): 699–720.

Bartlett, Bruce. 2007. "Starve the Beast": Origins and Development of a Budgetary Metaphor. *The Independent Review* XII (1): 5–26.

Bartolini, Leonardo, and Amartya Lahiri. 2006. Twin Deficits, Twenty Years Later. *Current Issues in Economics and Finance* 12 (7): 1–7.

Bator, Francis. 1965. Memorandum from the President's Deputy Special Assistant for National Security Affairs (Bator) to President Johnson. Washington, May 11, 1966, 5:45 p.m. In *Lyndon B. Johnson Library, National Security File, Subject File, Balance of Payments, Vol. 3 [1 of 2], Box 2. Secret; Sensitive.*

Baumgartner, Frank R., Christian Breunig, Christoffer Green-Pedersen, Bryan D. Jones, Peter B. Mortensen, Michiel Nuytemans, and Stefaan Walgrave. 2009. Punctuated Equilibrium in Comparative Perspective. *American Journal of Political Science* 53 (3): 603–620.

Baumgartner, Frank R., and Bryan D. Jones. 1993. *Agendas and Instability in American Politics*. Chicago: University of Chicago Press.

Bayard, Thomas O., and Kimberly Ann Elliott. 1994. *Reciprocity and Retaliation in U.S. Trade Policy*. Washington, DC: Institute for International Economics.

Bayoumi, Tamim, and Andrew Swiston. 2010. The Ties that Bind: Measuring International Bond Spillovers Using Inflation-Indexed Bond Yields. *IMF Staff Papers* 57 (2): 366–406.

Beecher, William. 1968. High Pentagon Aides Urge Call-up of 30,000 Men. *New York Times*, March 13, 1968, p. 15.

Belasco, Amy. 2009. *Troop Levels in the Afghan and Iraq Wars, FY2001-FY2012: Cost and Other Potential Issues*. Washington, DC: Congressional Research Service. R40682.

Berger, Henry W. 1975. Bipartisanship, Senator Taft, and the Truman Administration. *Political Science Quarterly* 90 (2): 221–237.

Bernanke, Ben. 2005. Remarks by Governor Ben S. Bernanke: The Global Saving Glut and the U.S. Current Account Deficit. *The Sandbridge Lecture, Virginia Association of Economists.*

Bernanke, Ben S., Carol Bertaut, Laurie Pounder DeMarco, and Steven Kamin. 2011. International Capital Flows and the Returns to Safe Assets in the United States, 2003–2007. Board of Governors of the Federal Reserve System International Finance Discussion Papers Number 1014.

Bernstein, Barton J. 1989. The Truman Administration and the Korean War. In *The Truman Presidency*, ed. Michael J. Lacy, pp. 410–444. Cambridge: Cambridge University Press.

Binder, Sarah A. 1999. The Dynamics of Legislative Gridlock, 1947–96. *American Political Science Review* 93 (3): 519–533.

2003. *Stalemate: Causes and Consequences of Legislative Gridlock.* Washington, DC: Brookings Institution Press.

Blanchard, Olivier, and Roberto Perotti. 2002. An Empirical Characterization of the Dynamic Effects of Changes in Government Spending and Taxes on Output. *The Quarterly Journal of Economics* 117 (4): 1329–1368.

Blinder, Alan S. 2013. *After the Music Stopped: The Financial Crisis, the Response, and the Work Ahead.* New York: Penguin.

Bluedorn, John, and Daniel Leigh. 2011. Revisiting the Twin Deficits Hypothesis: The Effect of Fiscal Consolidation on the Current Account. *IMF Economic Review* 59 (4): 582–602.

Board of Governors of the Federal Reserve System. 2012. *Flow of Funds Accounts of the United States: Annual Flows and Outstandings.*

2013. Foreign Exchange Rates. Retrieved from http://www.federalreserve.gov/releases/h10/summary/indexbc_m.htm (Accessed January 17, 2013).

Bordo, Michael, and Olivier Jeanne. 2002. Boom-Busts in Asset Prices, Economic Instability, and Monetary Policy. NBER Working Paper 8966. Cambridge, MA: National Bureau of Economic Research.

Bown, Chad P., and Meredith A. Crowley. 2013. Import Protection, Business Cycles, and Exchange Rates: Evidence from the Great Recession. *Journal of International Economics* 90 (1): 50–64.

Boyd, John H., and Mark Gertler. 1994. The Role of Large Banks in the Recent U.S. Banking Crisis. *Federal Reserve Bank of Minneapolis Quarterly Review* 18 (1): 2–21.

Brooks, Stephen G, G John Ikenberry, and William C Wohlforth. 2013. Don't Come Home, America: The Case against Retrenchment. *International Security* 37 (3): 7–51.

Brune, Lester H. 1989. Guns and Butter: The Pre-Korean War Dispute over Budget Allocations: Nourse's Conservative Keynesianism Loses Favor against Keyserling's Economic Expansion Plan. *American Journal of Economics and Sociology* 48 (3): 357–371.

Bundy, McGeorge. 1965. Memorandum from the President's Special Assistant for National Security Affairs (Bundy) to President Johnson, February 7, 1965. In *Foreign Relations of the United States, 1964–68*, Vol. 11, pp. 174–185. Washington, DC: Department of State.

Burnside, Craig, Martin Eichenbaum, and Jonas Fisher. 2004. Fiscal Shocks and their Consequences. *Journal of Economic Theory* 115 (1): 89–117.

Butler, Alison. 1991. Trade Imbalances and Economic Theory: The Case of the US-Japan Trade Deficit. *Federal Reserve Bank of St. Louis* (March/April): 16–31.

Calleo, David. 1982. *The Imperious Economy.* Cambridge, MA: Harvard University Press.

1992. *The Bankrupting of America.* New York: Morrow.

2009. *Follies of Power: America's Unipolar Fantasy.* New York: Cambridge University Press.

2010. American Decline Revisited. *Survival* 52 (4): 215–227.

Calvo, Guillermo A., Leonardo Leiderman, and Carmen M. Reinhart. 1993. Capital Inflows and Real Exchange Rate Appreciation in Latin America: The Role of External Factors. *IMF Staff Papers* 40 (1): 108–151.

Cao, Emily Yixuan, Yong Cao, Rashmi Prasad, and Zhengping Shen. 2011. US-China Exchange Rate Negotiation: Stakeholders, Participation and Strategy Deployment. *Business and Politics* 13 (3): 6.

Case, Karl E. 1991. The Real Estate Cycle and the Economy: Consequences of the Massachusetts Boom of 1984–1987. *New England Economic Review* (September/October): 37–46.

1994. Land Prices and House Prices in the United States. In *Housing Markets in the U.S. and Japan*, eds. Yukio Noguchi and James Poterba, pp. 29–48. Chicago: University of Chicago Press.

Cassing, James, Timothy J. McKeown, and Jack Ochs. 1986. The Political Economy of the Tariff Cycle. *The American Political Science Review* 80 (September): 843–862.

Chey, Hyoung-kyu. 2012. Theories of International Currencies and the Future of the World Monetary Order. *International Studies Review* 14 (1): 51–77.

Chinn, Menzie D. 2005. Getting Serious About the Twin Deficits. New York: Council on Foreign Relations.

Chinn, Menzie D., and Jeffrey A. Frieden. 2011. *Lost Decades: The Making of America's Debt Crisis and the Long Recovery.* New York: W. W. Norton.

Chinn, Menzie D., and Ito Hiro. 2008. Global Current Account Imbalances: American Fiscal Policy versus East Asian Savings. *Review of International Economics* 16 (3): 479–498.

Claessens, Stijn, Giovanni Dell'Ariccia, Deniz Igan, and Luc Laeven. 2010. Lessons and Policy Implications from the Global Financial Crisis. WP/10/44. Washington, DC: International Monetary Fund.

Claessens, Stijn, and M. Ayhan Kose. 2013. Financial Crises: Explanations, Types, and Implications. Washington, DC: International Monetary Fund.

Claessens, Stijn, M. Kose, Luc Laeven, and Fabián Valencia. 2013. Understanding Financial Crises: Causes, Consequences, and Policy Responses. Koç University-Tüsiad Economic Research Forum Working Paper 1301.

Clarida, Richard. 2005. Japan, China, and the U.S. current account deficit. *CATO Journal* 25 (1):111–114.

Cohen, Benjamin J. 2006. The Macrofoundations of Monetary Power. In *International Monetary Power*, ed. David Andrews, pp. 31–50. Ithaca, NY: Cornell University Press.

Collins, Robert M. 1996. The Economic Crisis of 1968 and the Waning of the "American Century." *The American Historical Review* 101 (2): 396–422.

Congressional Budget Office. 2013. *Estimated Impact of the American Recovery and Reinvestment Act on Employment and Economic Output from October 2012 Through December 2012.*

Corsetti, G., and G. J. Mueller. 2006. Twin Deficits: Squaring Theory, Evidence and Common Sense. *Economic Policy* 48: 598–638.

Costinot, Arnaud 2009. Jobs, Jobs, Jobs: A "New" Perspective on Protectionism. *Journal of the European Economic Association* 7 (5): 1011–1041.

Council of Economic Advisors. 2006. *Economic Report of the President*.

Creswell, John W, and Vicki L Plano Clark. 2010. *Designing and Conducting Mixed Methods Research*. Thousand Oaks, CA: SAGE.

Cusack, Thomas R., and Michael D. Ward. 1981. Military Spending in the United States, Soviet Union, and People's Republic of China. *Journal of Conflict Resolution* 25: 429–469.

D'Agostino, Brian. 1995. Self-Images of Hawks and Doves: A Control Systems Model of Militarism. *Political Psychology* 16 (2): 259–295.

Dao, James. 2001a. Democrats Say Bush's Tax Cuts Jeopardize Military Spending. *New York Times*, July 11, p. A14.

——— 2001b. Military Budget Creates Rift in G.O.P.: Fiscal Conservatives Clash with Advocates of Weapons Buildup. *New York Times*, July 26, p. A18.

Darvas, Zsolt 2012. Real Effective Exchange Rates for 178 Countries: A New Database. Working Paper 2012/06. Brussels: Bruegel.

Davis, Jack. 1996. Paul Wolfowitz on Intelligence-Policy Relations. *Studies of Intelligence* 39 (5): 35–42.

Dell'Ariccia, G., D. Igan, L. Laeven, and H. Tong. 2013. Policies for Macrofinancial Stability: Dealing with Credit Booms and Busts. In *Financial Crises, Consequences, and Policy Responses*, eds. S. Claessens, M. A. Kose, L. Laeven, and F. Valencia, pp. 365–396. Washington, DC: International Monetary Fund.

Dennis, Steven T. 2007. Budget Debate's Opening Statement. *CQ Weekly Online*, February 12, pp. 460–467.

Destler, I. M. 1991. U.S. Trade Policy-making in the Eighties. In *Politics and Economics in the Eighties*, eds. Alberto Alesina and Geoffrey Carliner, pp. 251–284. Chicago: University of Chicago Press.

——— 1995. *American Trade Politics*, 3rd ed. Washington, DC: Institute for International Economics.

——— 2005. *American Trade Politics*, 4th ed. Washington, DC: The Institute for International Economics.

Diamond, John M. 2008. *The CIA and the Culture of Failure*. Palo Alto: Stanford University Press.

Donovan, Robert J. 1996. *Tumultuous Years: the Presidency of Harry S. Truman, 1949–1953*. Columbia: University of Missouri Press.

Doughton, Robert L. 1950a. Letter to C.A. Cannon, July 25, 1950. In *Robert Lee Doughton Papers, #2862, Southern Historical Collection, The Wilson Library, University of North Carolina at Chapel Hill*. Robert Lee Doughton Papers, #2862, Southern Historical Collection, The Wilson Library, University of North Carolina at Chapel Hill. Box 49, Folder 1749.

——— 1950b. Various Letters. In *Robert Lee Doughton Papers, #2862, Southern Historical Collection, The Wilson Library, University of North Carolina at Chapel Hill*. Box 48, Folder 1749.

Drazen, Allan. 2000. *Political Economy in Macroeconomics*. Princeton, NJ: Princeton University Press.

Drezner, Daniel W. 2014. *The System Worked: How the World Stopped Another Great Depression*. Oxford: Oxford University Press.

Dryden, Steve. 1995. *Trade Warriors: USTR and the American Crusade for Free Trade*. New York: Oxford University Press.

Edelberg, Wendy, Martin Eichenbaum, and Jonas D. M. Fisher. 1999. Understanding the Effects of a Shock to Government Purchases. *Review of Economic Dynamics* 2 (1): 166–206.

Ehrmann, M., and M. Fratzscher. 2005. Equal Size, Equal Role? Interest Rate Interdependence Between the Euro Area and the United States. *Economic Journal* 115 (October): 928–948.

Ehrmann, M., M. Fratzscher, and R. Rigobon. 2007. Stocks, Bonds, Money Markets and Exchange Rates: Measuring International Financial Transmission. NBER Working Paper 11166. Cambridge, MA: National Bureau of Economic Research.

———. 2011. Stocks, Bonds, Money markets and exchange rates: measuring international financial transmission. *Journal of Applied Econometrics* 26 (6): 948–974.

Eichengreen, Barry J. 2000. From Benign Neglect to Malignant Preoccupation: U.S. Balance of Payments Policy in the 1960s. *NBER Working Paper 7630*. Cambridge, MA: National Bureau of Economic Research.

———. 2011. *Exorbitant Privilege: The Rise and Fall of the Dollar and the Future of the International Monetary System*. New York: Oxford University Press.

Eikenberry, Karl W. 2013. Reassessing the All-Volunteer Force. *The Washington Quarterly* 36 (1): 7–24.

Erceg, Christopher J., Luca Guerrieri, and Christopher Gust. 2005. Expansionary Fiscal Shocks and the US Trade Deficit. *International Finance* 8 (3): 363–397.

Executive Office of the President of the United States. 1964. Notes of the Leadership Meeting, White House, August 4, 1964. In *Foreign Relations of the United States, 1964–68, Vol. I: Vietnam, pp. 615–621*. Washington, DC: Department of State.

Executive Office of the President of the United States. 1965a. Memorandum for the Record, White House Meeting on Vietnam, February 6, 1965. In *Foreign Relations of the United States, Vol. II: Vietnam, pp. 158–160*. Washington, DC: Department of State.

———. 1965b. Memorandum of Meeting with Joint Congressional Leadership, July 27, 1965. In *Foreign Relations of the United States, Vol. II: Vietnam, pp. 264–269*. Washington, DC: Department of State.

———. 1966. Lyndon B. Johnson Recording, Robert McNamara, May 7, 1966. Retrieved from http://millercenter.org/scripps/archive/presidentialrecordings/johnson/1966/05_1966 (Accessed September 25, 2014).

———. 2001. *Budget of the United States Government*.

Fair Currency Coalition. 2010. Our Members. Retrieved from http://faircurrency.org/members.html (Accessed June 27, 2013).

Farrell, John Aloysius. 2001. *Tip O'Neill and the Democratic Century*. Boston: Little, Brown, and Company.

Federal Deposit Insurance Corporation. 1997. *History of the 1980s: Lessons for the Future*, Vol. I. *An Examination of the Banking Crises of the 1980s and Early 1990s*.

Federal Deposit Insurance Corporation. 2006. Region by Region: Looking Ahead at Banking Conditions in 2007. *FDIC Outlook* (Winter): 1.

Federal Reserve System. 2007. *Statistical Supplement to the Federal Reserve Bulletin*.

Federation of American Scientists. 2014. Intelligence Resource Program. Retrieved from http://www.fas.org/irp/budget/index.html (Accessed June 23, 2014).

Financial Crisis Inquiry Commission. 2011. *The Financial Crisis Inquiry Report: Final Report of the National Commission on the Causes of the Financial and Economic Crisis in the United States*.

Flood, Robert P, and Peter M Garber. 1984. Collapsing Exchange-Rate Regimes: Some Linear Examples. *Journal of International Economics* 17 (1): 1–13.

Flores-Macias, Gustavo A., and Sarah E. Kreps. 2013. Political Parties at War: A Study of American War Finance, 1789–2010. *American Political Science Review* 7 (4): 833–848.

Fordham, Benjamin O. 1998. *Building the Cold War Consensus: The Political Economy of US National Security Policy 1949–1951*. Ann Arbor: University of Michigan Press.

  2007. The Evolution of Republican and Democratic Positions on Cold War Military Spending. *Social Science History* 31: 603–636.

Frankel, Jeffrey. 2006. Could the Twin Deficits Jeopardize US Hegemony? *Journal of Policy Modeling* 28 (6): 653–663.

Freeman, John R., John T. Williams, and Tse-min Lin. 1989. Vector Autoregression and the Study of Politics. *American Journal of Political Science* 33 (4): 842–877.

Frieden, Jeffry A. 1991. Invested Interests: The Politics of National Economic Policies in a World of Global Finance. *International Organization* 45 (Autumn): 425–451.

  1997. Monetary Populism in Nineteenth Century America: An Open Economy Interpretation. *Journal of Economic History* 57 (June): 367–395.

Fuerbringer, Jonathan. 1982. Democrat Seeking Signal by Reagan on Tax Program. *New York Times*, March 6, p. A1.

Funabashi, Yoichi. 1988. *Managing the Dollar: From the Plaza to the Louvre*. Washington, DC: Institute for International Economics.

Gaddis, John Lewis. 1982. *Strategies of Containment: A Critical Appraisal of Postwar American National Security Policy*. Oxford: Oxford University Press.

Gallarotti, Giulio M. 1985. Toward a Business-Cycle Model of Tariffs. *International Organization* 39 (Winter): 155–187.

Gavin, Francis J. 2004. *Gold, Dollars, and Power: the Politics of International Monetary Relations, 1958–1971*. Chapel Hill: University of North Carolina Press.

Gavin, Michael, and Roberto Perrotti. 1997. Fiscal policy in Latin America. In *NBER Macroeconomics Annual 1997*, eds. B. Bernanke and J. Rotemberg, pp. 11–71. Cambridge, MA: MIT Press.

Gerdrup, Karsten R. 2003. Three Episodes of Financial Fragility in Norway since the 1890s. BIS Working Paper 142.

Gibbons, William Conrad. 1994. *The U.S. Government and the Vietnam War: Executive and Legislative Roles and Relationships*. Washington, DC: Government Printing Office.

Gilpin, Robert. 1981. *War and Change in World Politics*. Cambridge: Cambridge University Press.

Glad, Betty. 2009. *An Outsider in the White House: Jimmy Carter, His Advisors, and the Making of American Foreign Policy*. Ithaca, NY: Cornell University Press.

Gleditsch, Kristian Skrede. 2004. A Revised List of Wars Between and Within Independent States, 1816–2002. *International Interactions* 30: 231–262.

Goldstein, Joshua S. 2011. *Winning the War on War: The Decline of Armed Conflict Worldwide*. New York: Plume.

Gourinchas, Pierre-Olivier, Rodrigo Valdes, and Oscar Landerretche. 2001. Lending Booms: Latin America and the World. *Economia* (Spring): 47–99.

Grilli, Enzo. 1988. Macro-economic Determinants of Trade Protection. *The World Economy* 11 (3): 313–326.

Haass, RIchard N. 2013. *Foreign Policy Begins at Home: The Case for Putting America's House in Order*. New York: Basic Books.

Havens, Harry S. 1986. Gramm-Rudman-Hollings: Origins and Implementation. *Public Budgeting & Finance* 6 (3): 4–24.

Helleiner, Eric. 2008. Political Determinants of International Currencies: What Future for the US Dollar? *Review of International Political Economy* 15 (3): 354–378.

———. 2011. Understanding the 2007–2008 Global Financial Crisis: Lessons for International Political Economy. *Annual Review of Political Science* 14 (1): 67–87.

Helleiner, Eric, and Jonathan Kirshner, eds. 2009. *The Future of the Dollar*. Ithaca, NY: Cornell University Press.

Helleiner, Eric, Stefano Pagliari, and Hubert Zimmerman, eds. 2010. *Global Finance in Crisis: The Politics of International Regulatory Change*. London: Routledge.

Heo, Uk. 2010. The Relationship between Defense Spending and Economic Growth in the United States. *Political Research Quarterly* 63 (4): 760–770.

Herring, Richard, and Susan Wachter. 2003. "Bubbles in real estate markets." In *Asset Price Bubbles: The Implications for Monetary, Regulatory, and International Policies*, eds. William C. Hunter, George G. Kaufman, and Michael Pomerleano, pp. 217–257. Cambridge, MA: MIT Press.

Hufbauer, Gary Clyde, Yee Wong, and Ketki Sheth. 2006. *US-China Trade Disputes: Rising Tide, Rising Stakes*. Policy Analysis in International Economics Vol. 78. Washington, DC: Peterson Institute for International Economics.

Hung, Juann, Charles Pigott, and Anthony Rodrigues. 1989. Financial Implications of the U.S. External Deficit. *FRBNY Quarterly Review* 13 (4): 33–51.

International Monetary Fund. 2006. *Global Financial Stability Report, September*. Washington, DC: The International Monetary Fund.

Jervis, Robert. 1976. *Perception and Misperception in International Politics.* Princeton, NJ: Princeton University Press.

Johnson, Lyndon B. 1967. *President Lyndon B. Johnson 's Annual Message to the Congress on the State of the Union January 10, 1967.*

———. 1971. *The Vantage Point: Perspectives of the Presidency, 1963–1969.* New York: Holt, Rinehart and Winston.

Johnson, Simon, and James Kwak. 2010. *13 Bankers: The Wall Street Takeover and the Next Financial Meltdown.* New York: Pantheon.

Jones, Bryan D., and Frank Baumgartner. 2005. A Model of Choice for Public Policy. *Journal of Public Administration Research and Theory* 15 (3): 325–351.

Jones, Bryan D., Frank R. Baumgartner, Christian Breunig, Christopher Wlezien, Stuart Soroka, Martial Foucault, Abel Francois, Christoffer Green-Pedersen, Chris Koski, Peter John, Peter B. Mortensen, Frederic Varone, and Stefaan Walgrave. 2009. A General Empirical Law of Public Budgets: A Comparative Analysis. *American Journal of Political Science* 53 (4): 855–873.

Justiniano, Alejandro, Giorgio Primiceri, and Andrea Tambalotti. 2013. The Effects of the Saving and Banking Gluts on the US Economy. NBER Working Paper 19635. Cambridge, MA: National Bureau of Economic Research.

Kagan, Robert, and William Kristol. 2001. No Defense. *The Weekly Standard,* July 23, p. 11.

Kaminsky, Graciela L., and Carmen M. Reinhart. 1999. The Twin Crises: The Causes of Banking and Balance-Of-Payments Problems. *The American Economic Review* 89 (3): 473–500.

Kaminsky, Graciela L., Carmen M. Reinhart, and Carlos A. Végh. 2005. When It Rains, It Pours: Procyclical Capital Flows and Macroeconomic Policies. In *NBER Macroeconomics Annual 2004,* eds. Mark Gertler and Kenneth Rogoff, pp. 11–82. Cambridge: NBER Press.

Kawai, Masahiro. 1995. Accumulation of Net External Assets in Japan. In *Japan, Europe, and International Financial Markets: Analytical and Empirical Perspectives,* eds. Ryuzo Sato, Rama V. Ramachandran, and Richard M. Levich, pp. 73–123. Cambridge: Cambridge University Press.

Kennedy, Paul. 1987. *The Rise and Fall of Great Powers.* New York: Random House.

Kindleberger, Charles P., and Robert Z. Aliber. 2005. *Manias, Panics, and Crashes: A History of Financial Crises,* 5th ed. New York: John Wiley & Sons.

King, Ronald F. 1985. The President & Fiscal Policy in 1966: The Year Taxes Were Not Raised. *Polity* 17 (4): 685–714.

Kinsella, David. 1990. Defence Spending and Economic Performance in the United States: A Causal Analysis. *Defence Economics* 1 (4): 295–309.

Klarner, Carl E., Justin H. Phillips, and Matt Muckler. 2012. Overcoming Fiscal Gridlock: Institutions and Budget Bargaining. *The Journal of Politics* 74 (4): 992–1009.

Krippner, Greta R. 2011. *Capitalizing on Crisis: The Political Origins of the Rise of Finance.* Cambridge, MA: Harvard University Press.

Krugman, Paul. 1979. A Model of Balance-of-Payments Crises. *Journal of Money, Credit and Banking* 11 (3): 311–325.

———. 1985. Is the Strong Dollar Sustainable? In *The U.S. Dollar – Recent Developments, Outlook, and Policy Options*, ed. Federal Reserve Bank of Kansas City, pp. 3–16. Kansas City: Federal Reserve Bank of Kansas City.

———. 2007a. *The Conscience of a Liberal*. New York: W. W. Norton.

———. 2007b. Will There Be a Dollar Crisis? *Economic Policy* (July): 435–467.

Laeven, Luc, and Fabian Valencia. 2010. Resolution of Banking Crises: The Good, the Bad, and the Ugly. IMF Working Paper. Washington, DC: International Monetary Fund.

Lake, David A. 2011. Why "isms" Are Evil: Theory, Epistemology, and Academic Sects as Impediments to Understanding and Progress. *International Studies Quarterly* 55 (2): 465–480.

———. 2013. Theory Is Dead, Long Live Theory: The End of the Great Debates and the Rise of Eclecticism in International Relations. *European Journal of International Relations* 19 (3): 567–587.

Lambelet, John C. 1973. Towards a Dynamic Two-Theater Model of the East-West Arms Race. *Journal of Peace Science* 1 (1): 1–38.

Layne, Christopher. 2011. The Unipolar Exit: Beyond the Pax Americana. *Cambridge Review of International Affairs* 24 (2): 149–164.

———. 2012. This Time It's Real: The End of Unipolarity and the Pax Americana. *International Studies Quarterly* 56 (1): 203–213.

Leffler, Melvyn P. 1983. From the Truman Doctrine to the Carter Doctrine: Lessons and Dilemmas of the Cold War. *Diplomatic History* 7 (4): 245–266.

LeLoup, Lance T. 2005. *Parties, Rules, and the Evolution of Congressional Budgeting*. Columbus: Ohio State University Press.

LeLoup, Lance T., and John Hancock. 1988. Congress and the Reagan Budgets: An Assessment. *Public Budgeting & Finance* 8 (3): 30–54.

Majeski, Stephen. 1989. A Rule Based Model of the United States Military Expenditure Decision Making Process. *International Interactions* 15 (2): 129–154.

Mann, Thomas E., and Norman J. Ornstein. 2012. *It's Even Worse Than It Looks: How the American Constitutional System Collided with the New Politics of Extremism*. New York: Basic Books.

Marris, Stephen N. 1985. The Decline and Fall of the Dollar: Some Policy Issues. *Brookings Papers on Economic Activity* 1985 (1): 237–244.

Mason, David S. 2009. *The End of the American Century*. Lanham, MD: Rowman & Littlefield.

Mastanduno, Michael. 2009. System Maker and Privilege Taker: U.S. Power and the International Political Economy. *World Politics* 61 (1): 121–154.

Mayhew, David R. 2005. Wars and American Politics. *Perspectives on Politics* 3 (3): 473–493.

McCarthy, Jonathan, and Richard W Peach. 2004. Are Home Prices the Next Bubble? *FRBNY Economic Policy Review* 10 (3): 1–17.

McCarty, Nolan, Keith T. Poole, and Howard Rosenthal. 2013. *Political Bubbles: Financial Crises and the Failure of American Democracy*. Princeton, NJ: Princeton University Press.

McCubbins, Matthew D. 1991. Party Governance and U. S. Budget Deficits: Divided Government and Fiscal Stalemate. In *Politics and Economics in the Eighties*, eds. Alberto Alesina and Geoffrey Carliner, pp. 83–122. Chicago: University of Chicago Press.

McKeown, Timothy J. 1984. Firms and Tariff Regime Change: Explaining the Demand for Protection. *World Politics* 36 (January): 215–233.

Mendoza, Enrique G., and Marco E. Terrones. 2008. An Anatomy Of Credit Booms: Evidence From Macro Aggregates and Micro Data. NBER Working Paper 14049. Cambridge, MA: National Bureau of Economic Research.

1972. Financial Instability Revisited: The Economics of Disaster. *Reappraisal of the Federal Reserve Discount Mechanism* 3: 97–136.

Minsky, Hyman. 1977. The Financial Instability Hypothesis. *Challenge* (March/April): 20–27.

1986. *Stabilizing an Unstable Economy*. New Haven, CT: Yale University Press.

Minsky, Hyman P., and Henry Kaufman. 2008. *Stabilizing an Unstable Economy*, Vol. 1. New York: McGraw-Hill.

Mintz, Alex. 1992. *The Political Economy of Military Spending in the United States*, ed. Alex Mintz. London: Routledge.

Modigliani, Andre. 1972. Hawks and Doves, Isolationism and Political Distrust: An Analysis of Public Opinion on Military Policy. *The American Political Science Review* 66 (3): 960–978.

Moll, Kendall D., and Gregory M. Luebbert. 1980. Arms Race and Military Expenditure Models: A Review. *The Journal of Conflict Resolution* 24 (1): 153–185.

Morgan, Clifton, Navin Bapat, Valentin Krustev, and Yoshiharu Kobayashi. 2013. Threat and Imposition of Sanctions (TIES) Data 4.0 Users Manual Case Level Data. Retrieved from http://www.unc.edu/~bapat/tiesusersmanu-alv4.pdf (Accessed September 25, 2014).

Moschella, Manuela, and Eleni Tsingou. 2013. Regulating Finance after the Crisis: Unveiling the Different Dynamics of the Regulatory Process. *Regulation & Governance* 7 (4): 407–416.

Mosley, Layna, and David Singer. 2009. The Global Financial Crisis: Lessons and Opportunities for International Political Economy. *International Interactions* 35 (4): 420–429.

Moynihan, Daniel Patrick. 1985. Reagan's Inflate-the-Deficit Game: The Driving Motive Has Been to Dismantle 50 Years' Social Legislation." *New York Times*, July 21, p. E21.

Narizny, Kevin. 2007. *The Political Economy of Grand Strategy*. Ithaca, NY: Cornell University Press.

Nash, Nathaniel. 1988. American Shakeout in the Darwinian Age of Global Finance, Only Megabanks May Survive. *New York Times*, June 26, p. E1.

New York Times. 1968a. Clifford Orders Inquiry on Leaks. *New York Times*, March 24, p. 9.

1968b. "Wheeler to Brief Johnson on His Vietnam Trip Today." *New York Times*, February 28, p. 28.

Nincic, Miroslav, and Thomas R. Cusack. 1979. The Political Economy of U.S. Military Spending. *Journal of Peace Research* 16 (2): 101–115.

Oatley, Thomas. 2010. Exchange Rate Movements and the Demand for Protection. *Business and Politics* 12 (12): 1–16.

Oatley, Thomas, William K. Winecoff, Andrew Pennock, and Sarah Bauerle Danzman. 2013. The Political Economy of Global Finance: A Network Model. *Perspectives on Politics* 11 (1): 133–153.

Obstfeld, Maurice, and Kenneth Rogoff. 2007. The Unsustainable US Current Account Position Revisited. In *G7 Current Account Imbalances: Sustainability and Adjustment*, ed. Richard H. Clarida, pp. 339–366. Chicago: University of Chicago Press.

2009. Global Imbalances and the Financial Crisis: Products of Common Causes. In *Federal Reserve Bank of San Francisco Asia Economic Policy Conference*. Santa Barbara, CA.

Office of Management and Budget. 2004. *Overview of the President's 2005 Budget.*

O'Neill, Tip. 1987. *Man of the House.* New York: Random House.

Ostrom, Charles W., and Robin F. Marra. 1986. U.S. Defense Spending and the Soviet Estimate. *The American Political Science Review* 80 (3): 819–842.

Otero-Iglesias, Miguel, and Federico Steinberg. 2012. Is the Dollar Becoming a Negotiated Currency? Evidence from the Emerging Markets. *New Political Economy* 18 (3): 309–336.

2013. Reframing the Euro vs. Dollar Debate through the Perceptions of Financial Elites in Key Dollar-holding Countries. *Review of International Political Economy* 20 (1): 180–214.

Pape, Robert. 2009. Empire Falls. *National Interest*, January 22, p. 21.

Pew Research Center. 2011. *The Military-Civilian Gap: War and Sacrifice in the Post-9/11 Era.* Washington, DC: Pew Research Center, Social & Demographic Trends.

Phillips, Kate. 2009. Senate Approves Select Panel to Investigate Financial Crisis. April 22. Retrieved from http://thecaucus.blogs.nytimes.com/2009/04/22/senate-approves-select-panel-to-investigate-financial-crises (Accessed October 14, 2009).

Pierpaoli, Paul G. 1999. *Truman and Korea: The Political Culture of the Early Cold War.* Columbia, MO: University of Missouri Press.

Pinker, Stephen. 2012. *The Better Angels of our Nature: Why Violence Has Declined.* New York: Penguin.

Pollard, Robert A. 1989. The National Security State Reconsidered: Truman and Economic Containment, 1945–1950. In *The Truman Presidency*, ed. Michael J. Lacy, pp. 205–234. Cambridge: Cambridge University Press.

Prasad, Monica. 2012. The Popular Origins of Neoliberalism in the Reagan Tax Cut of 1981. *Journal of Policy History* 24 (3): 351–383.

Preble, Christopher. 2005. The Uses of Threat Assessment in Historical Perspective: Perception, Misperception and Political Will. Princeton, NJ: Princeton University Press. Retrieved from https://www.princeton.edu/~ppns/papers/Preble.pdf (Accessed September 25, 2104).

Rajan, Raghuram. 2005. Global Current Account Imbalances: Hard Landing or Soft Landing. March 15. Retrieved from http://www.imf.org/external/np/speeches/2005/031505.htm (Accessed November 3, 2010).

Ramey, Valerie A. 2011. Identifying Government Spending Shocks: It's All in the Timing. *The Quarterly Journal of Economics* 126 (1): 1–50.

——— 2012. Research. Retrieved from http://weber.ucsd.edu/~vramey/research. html-data (Accessed January 15, 2013).

Ramey, Valerie A., and Matthew D. Shapiro. 1998. Costly Capital Reallocation and the Effects of Government Spending. *Carnegie-Rochester Conference Series on Public Policy* 48: 145–194.

Reinhart, Carmen M., and Vincent R. Reinhart. 2009. Capital Flow Bonanzas: An Encompassing View of the Past and Present. In *NBER International Seminar in Macroeconomics 2008*, eds. Jeffrey Frankel and Francesco Giavazzi, pp. 9–62. Chicago: Chicago University Press.

Reinhart, Carmen, and Kenneth Rogoff. 2008a. Banking Crises: An Equal Opportunity Menace. NBER Working Paper 14587. Cambridge, MA: National Bureau of Economic Research.

——— 2008b. Is the 2007 US Sub-Prime Financial Crisis So Different? An International Historical Comparison. *American Economic Review* 98 (2):339–344.

Richardson, J. David. 1994. Trade Policy. In *American Economic Policy in the 1980s*, ed. Martin Feldstein, pp. 636–658. Chicago: University of Chicago Press.

Richardson, Lewis F. 1960. *Arms and Insecurity*. Pittsburgh: Boxwood.

Romer, Christina, and David Romer. 2008. *A Narrative Analysis of Postwar Tax Changes*. University of California, Berkeley. Retrieved from http://eml.berkeley.edu/~dromer/papers/nadraft609.pdf (Accessed September 25, 2014).

Rose, Andrew K. 2013. The March of an Economic Idea? Protectionism Isn't Counter-Cyclic (anymore). *Economic Policy* 28 (76): 569–612.

Roubini, Nouriel, and Stephen Mihm. 2010. *Crisis Economics: A Crash Course in the Future of Finance*. New York: Penguin.

Roubini, Nouriel, and Brad Setser. 2005a. Will the Bretton Woods 2 Regime Unravel Soon? The Risk of a Hard Landing in 2005–2006. Presented at the Revived Bretton Woods System: A New Paradigm for Asian Development?, San Francisco.

——— 2005b. Will the Bretton Woods 2 Regime Unravel Soon? The Risk of a Hard Landing in 2005–2006. In *Revived Bretton Woods System: A New Paradigm for Asian Development?* San Francisco: Federal Reserve Bank of San Francisco. Retrieved from http://www.frbsf.org/economic-research/events/2005/february/bretton-woods-asian-development-cpbs/ (Accessed September 25, 2014).

Rubin, Irene. 2007. The Great Unraveling: Federal Budgeting, 1998–2006. *Public Administration Review* 67 (4): 608–617.

Schatz, Joseph J. 2004. Tax Cuts, Spending Limits Divide Deficit-Conscious Republicans. *CQ Weekly Online*, January 31, pp. 278–281.

Schick, Allen. 2003. *Bush's Budget Problem*. Paper prepared for Conference on the George W. Bush Presidency, Princeton University.

Schuler, Kate. 2005. GOP Senators Bolt on Medicaid Cuts. *CQ Weekly Online*, March 21, p. 721.

Schwab, Susan Carol. 1994. *Trade-offs: Negotiating the Omnibus Trade and Competitiveness Act*. Boston: Harvard Business School Press.

Schwartz, Herman. 2009. *Subprime Nation: American Power, Global Capital, and the Housing Bubble*. Ithaca, NY: Cornell University Press.

Seabrooke, Leonard, and Eleni Tsingou. 2010. Responding to the Global Credit Crisis: The Politics of Financial Reform. *British Journal of Politics and International Relations* 12 (2): 313–323.

Secretary of Defense. 1964a. *Memorandum From the Secretary of Defense (McNamara) to the President, March 16, 1964.*

Secretary of Defense. 1964b. *National Security Action Memorandum, No. 288, March 17, 1964.*

Shapiro, Ian. 2005. *The Flight from Reality in the Human Sciences*. Princeton, NJ: Princeton University Press.

Sil, Rudra, and Peter J Katzenstein. 2010. *Beyond Paradigms: Analytic Eclecticism in the Study of World Politics*. London: Palgrave Macmillan.

Skidmore, David. 1996. *Reversing Course: Carter's Foreign Policy, Domestic Politics, and the Failure of Reform*. Nashville: Vanderbilt University Press.

Smith, Gaddis. 1986. *Morality, Reason, and Power*. New York: Hill and Wang.

Smith, Margaret Hwang, and Gary Smith. 2006. Bubble, Bubble, Where's the Housing Bubble? *Brookings Papers on Economic Activity* 2006 (1): 1–67.

Stein, Janice Gross, ed. 2013. *Threat Perception in International Relations*, eds. L. Huddy, D. O. Sears and J. S. Levy, 2nd ed., pp. 1–24. Oxford: Oxford University Press.

Stock, James H., and Mark W. Watson. 2001. Vector Autoregressions. *The Journal of Economic Perspectives* 15 (4): 101–115.

Strange, Susan. 1989. Toward a Theory of Transnational Empire. In *Global Changes and Theoretical Challenges: Approaches to World Politics for the 1990s*, eds. Ernst-Otto Czempiel and James Rosenau, pp. 161–176. Lexington, MA: Lexington Books.

1998. *Mad Money: When Markets Outgrow Governments*. Ann Arbor: University of Michigan Press.

Takacs, Wendy. 1981. Pressures for Protectionism: An Empirical Analysis. *Economic Inquiry* 19 (4): 687–693.

Talvi, Ernesto, and Carlos A. Vegh. 2005. Tax Base Variability and Procyclical Fiscal Policy In Developing Countries. *Journal of Development Economics* 78 (1): 156–190.

Taylor, Andrew. 2004. GOP Budget Resolution Stalemate Bad News for Party's Tax Agenda. *CQ Weekly Online*, May 1, 1015–1016.

2005. Fiscal 2006 Plan Narrowly Adopted. *CQ Weekly Online*, May 2, p. 1148.

Taylor, John B. 2007. Housing and Monetary Policy. Presented at the Housing, Housing Finance, and Monetary Policy, Jackson Hole, Wyoming.

2009. *Getting Off Track: How Government Actions and Interventions Caused, Prolonged, and Worsened the Financial Crisis*. Palo Alto: Hoover Institution Press.

2010. Getting Back on Track: Macroeconomic Policy Lessons from the Financial Crisis. *Federal Reserve Bank of St. Louis Review* 92 (3): 165–76.

Terrones, Marco. 2004. Are Credit Booms in Emerging Markets a Concern? In *World Economic Outlook*, ed. International Monetary Fund, pp. 147–166. Washington, DC: International Monetary Fund.

The Franklin Project. 2013. A 21st Century National Service System: A Plan of Action. Aspen, CO: The Aspen Institute.

The White House. 2000. *A National Security Strategy for a Global Age.* Retrieved from http://history.defense.gov/resources/nss2000.pdf

Thompson, Helen. 2009. The Political Origins of the Financial Crisis: The Domestic and International Politics of Fannie Mae and Freddie Mac. *The Political Quarterly* 80 (1): 17–24.

Tolchin, Martin. 1982a. A Month's Budget Talks Finally Come to Naught. *New York Times*, April 30, p. A17.

——— 1982b. Reagan Aids Hear Budget Attacked from Both Parties. *New York Times*, February 10, p. A1.

Tornell, Aaron, and Frank Westermann. 2002. Boom-Bust Cycles in Middle Income Countries: Facts and Explanation. *IMF Staff Papers* 49: 111–155.

Towell, Pat. 2001. Defense Budget Boost 'in Play. *CQ Weekly*, July 14, 1682.

Trubowitz, Peter. 2011. *Politics and Strategy: Partisan Ambition and American Statecraft.* Princeton, NJ: Princeton University Press.

True, James L. 2009. Historical Budget Records Converted to the Present Functional Categorization with Actual Results for FY 1947–2008. Retrieved from http://www.policyagendas.org/page/datasets-codebooks#budget_authority_ (adjusted) (Accessed September 25, 2014).

Truman, Harry S. 1950. *Special Message to the Congress Reporting on the Situation in Korea, July 19.*

Tsingou, Eleni. 2010. Regulatory Reactions to the Global Credit Crisis: Analysing a Policy Community Under Stress. In *Global Finance in Crisis*, eds. Eric Helleiner, Stefano Pagliari, and Hubert Zimmerman, pp. 21–36. New York: Routledge.

U.S. Department of Commerce Census Bureau. 2010. Housing Starts: Total: New Privately Owned Housing Units Started. Retrieved from http://research.stlouisfed.org/fred2/data/HOUST.txt (Accessed September 25, 2014).

United States Department of Defense. 2014. Casualty. Retrieved from http://www.defense.gov/news/casualty.pdf (Accessed June 29, 2014).

United States Government. 1970. *The Report of the President's Commission on an All-Volunteer Armed Force.*

U.S. Department of State. 1998. *Foreign Relations of the United States, 1964–68: International Monetary and Trade Policy*, Vol. VIII. Washington, DC: Government Printing Office.

——— 2006. *Foreign Relations of the US, 1964–69: XXIX, Part 2 Japan.* Washington, DC: Government Printing Office.

Webb, Michael C. 1991. International Economic Structures, Government Interests, and International Coordination of Macroeconomic Adjustment policies. *International Organization* 45 (3): 309–342.

Weisman, Steven R. 1982. Reagan Rejects Advice to Alter Budget Proposal. *New York Times*, March 2, p. A1.

Wells, Samuel F., Jr. 1979. Sounding the Tocsin: NSC 68 and the Soviet Threat. *International Security* 4 (2): 116–158.

West, Darrell M. 1988. Gramm-Rudman-Hollings and the Politics of Deficit Reduction. *Annals of the American Academy of Political and Social Science* 499 (September): 90–100.

Whitney, Robert F. 1950. Tax Rise Effective at Once Is Urged by Taft, O'Mahoney. *New York Times*, July 24, p. 1.

Whitten, Guy D., and Laron K. Williams. 2011. Buttery Guns and Welfare Hawks: The Politics of Defense Spending in Advanced Industrial Democracies. *American Journal of Political Science* 55 (1): 117–134.

Wilson, James Q. 1991. *Bureaucracy: What Government Agencies Do and Why They Do It*. New York: Basic Books.

Yellen, Janet L. 1989. Symposium on the Budget Deficit. *The Journal of Economic Perspectives* 3 (2): 17–21.

Zeiler, Thomas W. 1992. *American Trade and Power in the 1960s*. New York: Columbia University Press.

Zelizer, Julian E. 2000. *Taxing America: Wilbur D. Mills, Congress, and the State, 1945–1975*. Cambridge: Cambridge University Press.

    2010. *Arsenal of Democracy: The Politics of National Security–from World War II to the War on Terrorism*. New York: Basic Books.

Zimmermann, Hubert. 1996. "… they have got to put something in the family pot! The Burden Sharing Problem in German-American Relations 1960–1967. *German History* 14 (3): 325–346.

    2002. *Money and Security: Troops, Monetary Policy, and West Germany's Relations with the United States and Britain, 1950–71*. Cambridge: Cambridge University Press.

Index

Ackley, Gardner, 73
adjustment
  deflection of, 125–126
  political economy of imbalance and,
    151–153
Afghanistan
  public involvement in, 163
  Soviet invasion of, 41–43, 52–56,
    73–74
  U.S. troops in, 150–151
aggregate demand, Mundell–Fleming
  open economy model, 87–89
all-volunteer military, shift to,
  163–164
al-Qaeda, attacks in U.S. by, 41–43,
  55–58
American Conservative Union, 74–75
American hegemony
  institutions and financial power
    and, 151–153
  military dimensions of, 3–6, 27–31
  political economy of imbalance and,
    150–165
  retrenchment and deficits and,
    157–161
American Home Mortgage, 141
American Recovery and Reinvestment
  Act (ARRA), 2–3
Americans for Democratic Action
  (ADA), 74–75
analytic eclecticism, political economy
  of imbalance and, 19–22
antidumping policies

correlates of deflection and,
    123–125
dollar valuation and, 113–119
pro-cyclicality of postwar
    protectionism and, 108–113
time series analysis of, 113–119
Arab-Israeli conflicts, 41–43
Arab oil embargo of 1973, 52–56
Art, Robert J., 150, 157
Aspen Institute, Franklin project of,
    164–165
asset bubbles
  banking crises and, 127–129,
    139–142
  capital market dynamics and, 13–14
  credit booms and, 129–132,
    136–139
  financial instability hypothesis and,
    154–157
  limits of financial regulation and,
    154–157
  postwar trends in, 132–146
  price deflation and, 139–142
attrition, wars of, bargaining
  environment for deficit reduction
  and, 68–73
Authorization for Use of
  Military Force Against Terrorists,
    57–58
automobile industry, economic booms,
  and protectionism for, 108–113
autonomy, financial power and,
    98–102